Strategic learning in action

THE HENLEY MANAGEMENT SERIES

Series Adviser: Professor Bernard Taylor

Also available in the McGraw-Hill/Henley Management Series:

MANAGING INFORMATION
Information systems for today's general manager
A V Knight and D J Silk   ISBN 0-07-707086-0

THE NEW GENERAL MANAGER
Confronting the key challenge of today's organizations
Paul Thorne   ISBN 0-07-707083-6

THE COMPETITIVE ORGANIZATION
Managing for organizational excellence
Gordon Pearson   ISBN 0-07-707480-7

TOTAL CAREER MANAGEMENT
Strategies for creating management careers
Frances A Clark   ISBN 0-07-707558-7

CREATING THE GLOBAL COMPANY
Successful internationalization
Colin Coulson-Thomas   ISBN 0-07-707599-4

THE HANDBOOK OF PROJECT-BASED MANAGEMENT
Improving the processes for achieving strategic objectives
Rodney Turner   ISBN 0-07-707656-7

CREATING EXCELLENCE IN THE BOARDROOM
A guide to shaping directorial competence and board effectiveness
Colin Coulson-Thomas   ISBN 0-07-707796-2

FINANCE FOR THE GENERAL MANAGER
A four-step approach to the key financial techniques
Roger Mills and Janine Stiles   ISBN 0-07-707960-4

Details of these and other titles in the series are available from:

The Product Manager, Professional Books, McGraw-Hill Book Company
Europe, Shoppenhangers Road, Maidenhead, Berkshire SL6 2QL
Telephone 0628 23432   Fax 0628 770224

Strategic learning in action

How to accelerate and sustain business change

Tony Grundy

McGRAW-HILL BOOK COMPANY

London · New York · St Louis · San Francisco · Auckland
Bogotá · Caracas · Lisbon · Madrid · Mexico · Milan
Montreal · New Delhi · Panama · Paris · San Juan
São Paulo · Singapore · Sydney · Tokyo · Toronto

Published by
McGRAW-HILL Book Company Europe
Shoppenhangers Road, Maidenhead, Berkshire SL6 2QL, England
Telephone 0628 23432
Fax 0628 770224

British Library Cataloguing in Publication Data

Grundy, Tony
   Strategic Learning in Action: How to
   Accelerate and Sustain Business Change. –
   (Henley Management Series)
   I. Title II. Series
   658.4012

   ISBN 0-07-707825-X

Library of Congress Cataloging-in-Publication Data

Grundy, Tony
   Strategic learning in action: how to accelerate and sustain
business change / Tony Grundy.
      p.   cm. – (The Henley management series)
   Includes bibliographical references and index.
   ISBN 0-07-707825-X
      1. Organizational change. 2. Organizational behavior.
   3. Organizational effectiveness.   I. Title.   II. Series.
   HD58.8.G78   1994
   658.4´06–dc20   94-10894
                                                                        CIP

12345 CUP 97654

Typeset by BookEns Limited, Baldock, Herts.
and printed and bound in Great Britain at the University Press, Cambridge

Contents

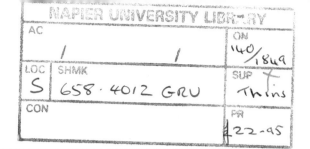

Preface

Why is this book needed?

Why do so many organizations fail whatever their size? Why is it that so many managers seem unable to manage complex change, to identify key sources of uncertainty, and to confront dilemmas in a strategic manner?

After the 1980s and early 1990s it seems as if Peters and Waterman ought to have entitled their book on *In Search of Incompetence* rather than *In Search of Excellence*. The very popularity of *The Survivors' Guides* to modern management since Peters and Waterman underscores the growing crisis in modern management. Like the ailing patient, managers may seek new wonder drugs to ameliorate their conditions, trying one new treatment after another (often giving none sufficient time to work) – they seem to fall victim to hypochondria.

A great many of these drugs have been available. In the 1970s there was marketing management and long-range planning. We then had, in quick succession, the cult of leadership and the upsurge in growth of strategic management. Then came customer care, total quality management, corporate mission and culture change. In the field of operations management, 'distribution' became 'logistics' overnight and business process redesign was born – with some resemblances to organization and methods (O&M). Unfortunately many of these useful additions to management practice have become tainted as passing fashions. This is often because these processes have not been well integrated, understood and owned by managers.

What does the book offer?

The position, however, may not be as hopeless as it seems. This book shows how it is possible to make management tools work for managers by integrating them with a learning process. Within this process managers carefully select the most powerful management tools. These tools are then brought together and applied to practical issues through an orchestrated learning process. This is illustrated by a number of major case studies, including Dowty, Mercury Communications, Shell and Interspace. You will also work through shorter case studies and through a series of self-diagnosis exercises.

This learning process is called 'strategic learning', thus highlighting how learning may help devise and implement strategy at corporate, business and individual levels; it also highlights how learning may identify wider patterns in what is happening outside the organization and challenge what is happening inside it. This involves taking a 'holistic view' of these issues. This is easily said, but is a lot harder to spread throughout the organization, and to sustain.

The word 'strategic' thus emphasizes that learning can become a more coherent and central set of processes in driving organizations forward. It also positions learning as a core and permanent concern of general management. In achieving its objectives the book examines differing notions of strategy and of learning, but moves on rapidly to deal with the application of strategic learning.

Strategic Learning in Action differs in many respects from earlier management books:

1. It does not pretend that there is a simple, single way of curing all (or most) of managers' problems. Strategic learning embraces a variety of frameworks and tools – it is the glue that holds them together.
2. It is not based on simplistic prescriptions that ignore the major issue of *implementation*. Unlike traditional strategic planning, which focuses mainly on analysis and decision-making, it deals directly with problems of creating action and managing change.
3. It takes a step-by-step approach to showing how strategic learning can form *the backbone of key management processes*. By making the learning imperative explicit within the organization, learning becomes a conscious and thereby more effective driver of management action.
4. Its style is one very much of *informing* and *arguing* instead of *prescribing* – its aim is to open up awareness to what is both possible and essential rather than to extol the impossible. Its style is therefore lively and rich in illustrations.

The book begins by explaining the idea of strategic learning and how it links to other key management ideas. Once this preparatory work has been achieved you will then be in a position to enjoy and learn from the main case studies and exercises at the core of the book.

What the book is and isn't

The book's primary contribution is not towards building radically new theories of management or organizational learning *per se*. Nor is it an attempt to prescribe new management ideals that are difficult, if not impossible, to implement – for instance, in putting forward the notion of the 'learning organization'. It deals instead with *applying* strategic learning – in action.

It is also not a comprehensive guide to corporate strategy, but readers will find some new angles on the strategic management process, on strategic thinking and on exploiting competitive strategy in practice.

The book explores the benefits of strategic learning from a variety of perspectives. First, it shows how strategic learning can play a major role in shaping the development of business strategy and help focus organizational change. Second, it can help achieve quantum improvements in organizational capability and performance. Third, it can be used as a vehicle for team and individual development. Fourth, it helps individuals and teams to map the complex issues and dynamics occurring within their organization. It may thereby deliver for them a personal competitive advantage by giving them the means to deal with ambiguity more effectively.

All of the above needs – business-wide and individual – can be fulfilled more effectively by consciously applying strategic learning to key issues for advantage. This can be achieved most directly through undertaking the case exercises within the book. They are of practical and personal relevance, have been well tested and, typically, yield many benefits, so do not be tempted to skim them.

Who is the book written for?

The book therefore fulfils an array of overlapping needs of the general manager, of the head of function, of the middle (line) manager and also of the internal and external developer/facilitator. Increasingly, the general and middle manager have a role in facilitating learning throughout the organization. Likewise, management and organization developers/facilitators have a role to play at the core of the management process, rather than out on the periphery.

The book also has a second role as a supporting text for students wishing to make more practical sense out of theories of strategic management, organizational behaviour and change, and therefore fills an important gap in bridging practice and theory.

Acknowledgements

I would like to thank Dave King and Nicky Burton (formerly of Dowty Communications), John Mittens and Russell Connor of Mercury Communications, Graham Galer of Shell and Alan Friend of J. Lyons for their invaluable help on the cases in this book. I would also like to thank Eric Gabriel and Alan Mumford for their comments on various drafts.

PART ONE
THE LEARNING
IMPERATIVE

1
Introduction

1.1　What is strategic learning?

In order to explore the notion of strategic learning, we shall start with a personal experience and turn to concepts later. We shall then return to this experience before putting forward a model of strategic learning.

Introductory case – Nebula International

Some years ago I worked as a consultant with a major consulting firm. During this time I made the mistake of taking a whole two weeks' holiday in North Yorkshire. While I was combating the coastal sea mist (at the same time as the rest of the country was baking in 30°C heat), my superiors were busy plotting my next six months' work.

I returned to my desk on Monday morning expecting to have a week on low-power. Instead, I found a note which read:

> Dear Tony,
> I expect you have had a most restful two weeks. I know how pleased you will be that we have found you another project to keep you out of the office. From 9 am tomorrow you will be (until further notice) the head of finance, planning and acquisitions for the fast-growing, £100m turnover division of a major multi-national, Nebula International.
> We know a bit about the assignment which I can share with you. However, their finance people have offered to tell you more about it so I guess a quick session with myself and the client partner will help you gain a good overview.
> Oh, you may need to pack, as it is over 100 miles from Cambridge. I am sure you will be able to negotiate adequate living costs from your new client.
> Best of luck, your Consulting Partner . . .

Most managers will recognize a typical 'mission impossible' assignment in the above. Yet the point of this example is to highlight the value of 'strategic learning' as follows. Imagine that you live through this experience as if it were your own next project.

In the first week of this assignment it becomes apparent that there are a number of major issues that need to be thought through:

1. Businesses in the UK, in Europe and in the US need in-depth, post-acquisition management.
2. Evaluation of major new acquisition targets is at the top of senior management's agenda.
3. A number of key R&D decisions need evaluating in the near future.
4. The medium-range plan for this growing division is required within three months but few, if any, preparations have been put in place for this.
5. Group head office are closely scrutinizing financial performance in the wake of earlier acquisitions – concern has been triggered due to a number of problem areas.
6. A new distribution channel needs absorbing as a result of a recent Group reorganization.
7. Changes in transfer pricing within the Group are imminent and need negotiating and planning. This will be a tricky exercise both technically and politically.
8. A drop in morale within the Finance and Planning Group has occurred and key members of your team are dispirited and exhausted following several months of working flat out.
9. Your own role needs to be defined more clearly (your job reports directly to the divisional MD with a dotted line to the finance director of another, larger division, based on the same site).

And so on.

Exercise 1.1 Prioritizing key issues (10 minutes)

Given the information available, which issues would you rank as being (a) most important, (b) most urgent? You may make assumptions as appropriate in order to complete this exercise.

A casual scan at the above list of issues highlights the range of difficult and urgent issues that needed to be faced. Despite obvious pressures for quick action, you opt to spend the first two or three weeks in intensive diagnosis, mapping how the various issues interrelate, and in initial planning. This intensive collection, analysis of, and reflection on data is in effect 'strategic learning', which it is now relevant to define.

Defining strategy, learning and strategic learning

'Strategy' has been defined in countless different ways which I do not propose to enumerate. If we can capture over 80 per cent of the meanings of the many definitions we shall have done well. We therefore define 'strategy' as:

> *A pattern in the decisions and behaviour of an organization, team or individual in creating or responding to change.*

This definition borrows from Mintzberg's idea of strategy as a 'pattern'[1] but leaves it open as to whether the pattern is conscious or subconscious, preplanned ('deliberate') or emergent. It also extends to behaviour as well as decisions.

Further, the definition covers not merely organizations but also teams and individuals. Finally, it is inextricably linked to *change*, whether this change is managed proactively or reactively. It leaves open whether the change is *designed* to secure competitive advantage[2] or not.

Learning can now be defined as follows:

> *A conscious or subconscious process of developing or adapting perspectives to make better sense of the world.*

This definition again allows for learning to be unconscious. It also links learning to the idea of making sense of both the external and internal environment.

Having defined 'strategy' and 'learning' we can now define strategic learning:

> *An open process of exploring complex and ambiguous issues affecting organizations, teams and individuals. This process involves reflecting and debating on the linkages, tensions and conflicts between issues and seeing these in the wider context.*

Strategic learning is thus about resolving issues that are notoriously messy rather than simple: these issues usually involve uncertainty, interdependence and, above all, handling dilemmas.[3]

Strategic learning (like the idea of 'strategy') can be applied at a variety of levels – for instance, in directing an organization, in seeking more effective team-working right down to defining the role of an individual. Unlike more conventional views of 'strategy', the 'issues' involved need not be at such a high level as, for instance, corporate strategy, but they will involve looking at issues in a wider context, beyond the immediate theatre of thinking or action.

Figure 1.1 is a pictorial display of the ingredients of strategic learning, and

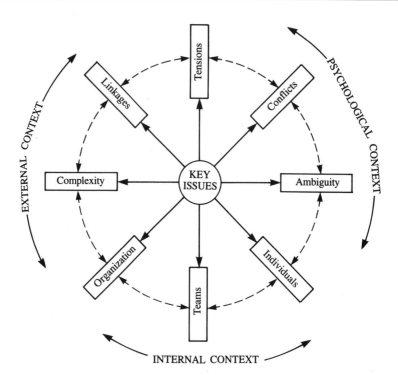

Figure 1.1 What is strategic learning?

shows not only how key issues are generated by complexity and ambiguity, but also how these impact at different levels – organization, teams, individual – and in different ways. The figure also highlights how these factors interact with one another and how they relate to the external, internal and psychological context.

The case continues

After this discussion on the nature of strategic learning, we return to the case to see how events unfolded. Following the first three weeks in your new role, you are able to better understand the key vulnerabilities, opportunities and interdependencies both within your own area of responsibility and relative to the wider context. By questioning and listening to your staff and to divisional management and key stakeholders elsewhere in the Group, you are able to network in your mind not just the business issues, but also the pressure points and how these can be managed. Most importantly, you relate these to the political interplay within the division and particularly to your dual reporting role: to the managing director and, functionally, to a finance director. A map of the key issues is shown in Figure 1.2, which highlights a cluster of issues associated with acquisitions and strategy, further problems of staff and organization, and some reporting problems. The illustrative process shown in Figure 1.2 is a very important element in strategic learning. Pictorial maps enable you to locate the worst problems and begin to diagnose why they appear so intractable, they may also suggest ways of unravelling problem knots.

With hindsight, a critical success factor lay in your identifying that taking up this new role involved a learning process. This involved your thinking and learning strategically at a business, organizational, team and personal level simultaneously.

By analysing these issues, and by understanding deeper and less obvious patterns in what was going on, you are able to integrate your team and, through their commitment, deliver solutions.

Phases of strategic learning: introducing SARTRE

A number of key phases within the learning process may be identified from the case:

1. *Surfacing*: ensuring that all the key 'hard' and 'soft' issues are identified.

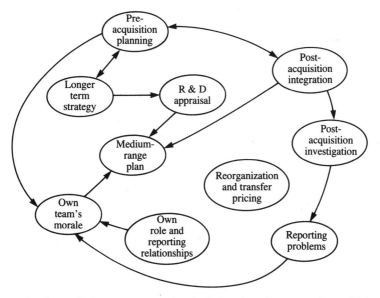

Figure 1.2 Strategic issues map – as head of planning, finance and acquisitions

2. *Analysing*: understanding how these issues interrelate, and what sub-issues are involved; then evaluating these in terms of urgency, importance, uncertainty and degree of difficulty.
3. *Reshaping*: searching for ways of resolving many issues or sub-issues in one pass; alternatively, breaking off sub-issues that can be dealt with separately; then searching for less obvious options that may redefine the problem.
4. *Targeting*: identifying the desired outputs – for instance, in terms of specific actions or changes.
5. *Resolving*: programming how this can be achieved within time and resource constraints.
6. *Experimenting*: taking first steps to see if the chosen path is workable and advantageous.

These six phases may be easily remembered via the acronym SARTRE (named, coincidentally, after the famous French philosopher).

In the earlier case (Nebula), which focused mainly on surfacing[4] and analysing, there were a number of immediate and tangible issues which, although large, were not necessarily the most difficult.

Let us now turn to the phases of reshaping, targeting and resolving. Resuming the Nebula case earlier, a recent major acquisition now requires closer inspection. However, the business is considered to be sound, its management considered solid, and the issues revolved mainly around avoiding damage via ill-thought-through integration. On the other hand, there are a number of difficult organizational issues which are at once urgent, important and uncertain. In particular, the morale of the planning and finance team is dropping. No real progress can be made on other issues until renewed confidence is gained.

Equally, your dual reporting issue proves to be a minefield. You now need to set about team-building so that both sides (the business's general management and the functional management within the division) realize they have very similar concerns that are not really so distant.

There are other lessons too from this case. Although your position was considered to be 'senior', this was more of an advisory rather than executive role. Even though the role was notionally head of planning in the hierarchy, it was not seen as a natural thing for you to challenge and question the business strategy, the way in which things were managed and how priorities were set.

But some amount of challenge is essential. As many middle managers find, managing upwardly sets more senior managers aback – at least, at first; but when they see that you are surfacing some major issues and suggesting how these might be resolved, a responsive organization quickly uses this positive challenge to advantage. Strategic learning is thus not a politics- or power-free process – it involves dealing with issues in which the political sensitivity can be very intense. Indeed, a crucial ingredient of strategic learning is the active analysis of power structures and influences – as well as the analysis of more concrete issues.

In the next section you will begin to explore how strategic learning can be used to advantage – at the business, the team or the individual level.

1.2 How can strategic learning help you?

Following on from the earlier case, you are now invited to analyse some of the issues which you face in your current role. This gives you a taste of the benefits of strategic learning. The following exercise should take you between 10 and 20 minutes. Try to draw your issues pictorially using a single sheet of A4. Do a quick, first effort and then redraw the map to cluster issues that are closely interrelated. By the third attempt you should have a good picture.

Exercise 1.2   Defining strategic issues (15 minutes)

Draw a strategic issue map as follows:

1. What are the key issues facing you in your role?
2. How do these map on to key issues facing your team, department, business?
3. What are the main linkages between these issues?
4. Does this map of issues suggest any central problem knots* that are difficult to resolve?
5. What overall patterns emerge from drawing up this picture? For example, where several difficult issues are closely interrelated, this may suggest a single thrust to deal with them all at the same time.

*A 'problem knot' is where many interrelationships between problems overlap and intertwine to produce a messy picture. This may highlight where the most serious problems lie, and also hint at where and how these can be unravelled. For instance, in Figure 1.2, the medium-range plan appears to be central in dealing with many other problems, yet this issue has been put on the back-burner while the team attends to apparently more pressing things.

Before we move on, let us review what you have learned from this exercise. You may have found that a number of issues that were peripheral to your previous thoughts now seem to be more central. They may seem marginal, but sometimes issues on the periphery turn out to be pivotal in resolving key problems.

You may also have found that one issue has emerged to be at the heart of your problems. This may be adjacent to an issue that was previously seen as unimportant. However, the core issue may involve a process, or softer management area. This is fairly typical: for example, a manager involved in a major downsizing in a large company identified that a critical issue was how the *criteria* for defining who was to stay versus who was to go should be communicated explicitly to staff. Here the *communication process* was perceived to be a more important issue than the actual content of the change.

Managers are often inhibited from drawing up maps of strategic issues owing to the fear that someone might 'see' what they are up to, or simply because of embarrassment. Naturally, you may wish to draw these issue maps up privately; however, unless you are prepared to share your insights, this may achieve only partial and purely personal strategic learning. The bulk of the practical benefit from strategic learning accrues not purely through personally related insights, but also through sharing issues with others.

Learning can therefore play a major role in analysing strategic issues, affecting the wider organization, particularly those at the heart of how competitive advantage is generated – a topic to which we now turn.

1.3   Integrating learning with competitive advantage

Learning in many organizations is, in the 1990s, still seen as something 'nice to do'. Even within those companies which have a focus on learning, this is rapidly abandoned at times of turbulence and crisis.

Learning is often associated with training and development activities, rather than being seen as *the* process that drives the organization on a day-to-day basis. Yet the practice of strategic learning can yield major improvements in tangible competitive advantage.

Case study 1.1 Tangible competitive advantage at Neptune Technology

In Neptune Technology, a fast-growing business, a small group of managers were asked to brainstorm areas where more revenue could be added, with the same or less cost. This was part of an exercise in 'strategic cost management' which considers cost to be a strategic rather than a primarily tactical issue. In strategic cost management financial benefits are seen as integral with competitive advantage.

After just 50 minutes of discussion and debate, the group of managers reported that they had identified additional net revenue potential of up to £2 million over the next four years. This related to customer service which had not been fully exploited and where customers were likely to pay for service enhancement. Previously the company had been unwilling to exploit this, because of perceived resource and financial constraints. Also no one had analysed what customers might pay for this service.

There are many other examples of the way in which strategic learning can add to competitive advantage. What had been previously lacking in this company was (a) the time to reflect on the issue, and (b) the realization that via strategic cost management some extra costs might be permissible in view of the extra value (and revenue) generated.

Strategic learning then needs to be in-built into organizational recipes and routines – indeed into the very heart of 'how we do things around here'. This involves a sustained campaign to demonstrate the benefits of strategic learning through a stream of successes, each bringing tangible advantages to the business.

1.4 How to use this book

This book contains a rich variety of material through which you can explore the potential of strategic learning. This is illustrated in Figure 1.3, which is a guide to the book.

First, we take a look at different approaches to *formal* strategic learning. This contrasts more conventional learning programmes with those that deal more directly with live organizational issues. This is of relevance both to those managers involved in the *design* of learning programmes and those who wish to self-manage their strategic learning – either as individuals or in small groups.

In Chapter 3 we turn to understanding the links between learning and competitive advantage. This may shed fresh light on key concepts in strategic management and in competitive strategy. By taking a *learning perspective* on this key area we are able to identify many of the underlying blocks to creating and sustaining competitive advantage. This chapter will thus be of particular interest to managers who want to apply new approaches to gain lasting breakthroughs in business performance. It will also be of interest to management and organization developers for whom the idea of competitive advantage seems to be lofty and dissociated from that of learning.

Part Two – 'Facilitating the learning process' – then moves back to how strategic learning is facilitated in practice. This gives clear guidance on how to experiment with strategic learning targeted at specific business problems or opportunities. This is further supported by cases (at Dowty and at Mercury Communications) where strategic learning has been used to steer

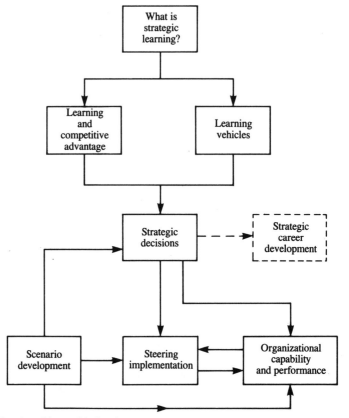

Figure 1.3   A guide to this book

the management process, either through strategic decision-making or in implementing change.

In the final part of the book we look at a 'Menu of strategic learning'. This covers scenario planning (at Shell) and also organizational capability and performance. Scenarios are useful in guiding strategic decisions and also in steering implementation (bottom centre of Figure 1.3). Organizational capability and performance are also very closely interrelated (bottom right of Figure 1.3).

We also come back to perhaps the most important focal point – yourself. A whole chapter is devoted to helping you understand your own position, capability and potential in a more strategic way. Finally, we conclude by reviewing how strategic learning interrelates and integrates management issues that you currently face.

References

1. Mintzberg, H., 'Patterns in strategy formation', *Management Science*, May 1978, pp. 934–48.
2. Porter, M. E., *Competitive Advantage*, The Free Press, New York, 1985.
3. Hampden Turner, C., *Charting the Corporate Mind*, Blackwell, 1990.
4. Mitroff, I. I. and Linstone, H. A., *The Unbounded Mind*, Oxford University Press, 1993.

2
Exploring strategic learning

2.1 Introduction

In our second chapter we explore in greater depth how strategic learning happens, and how it can be facilitated or impeded. This begins with an exercise for you to reflect upon some of your own recent business experiences, focusing especially on critical success factors. We then examine how learning can be impeded by fear of making errors (or having errors detected), illustrating this with problems of group learning – especially of groupthink.

In Section 2.3 we then look at different schools of thought on organizational learning, illustrating this with the Uranus case. In Section 2.4 we then build a framework for understanding how strategic learning works and explain the cycle of strategic learning.

The reasons why the process sometimes works and sometimes *doesn't* are then examined by calling on some recent research at Cranfield. In the Cranfield study managers sometimes achieved learning breakthroughs, sometimes were distracted, and sometimes found important learning insights drifting off their action agenda.

This chapter thus sets the scene for the learning process at work in core cases in later chapters.

2.2 Exercise: critical success factors

Many management books hit the reader with a deluge of tools, prescriptive ideas and theoretical frameworks. Yet this approach, which can be characterized as 'knowledge-push', flies in the face of what is known about management learning. For adults generally, and managers in particular, learning occurs mainly through 'experience-pull'.

Kolb[1] introduced the idea of a learning cycle, which begins with concrete experience, moves on into observation and reflection, then to abstract-reasoning and finally to testing on new experiences. These four stages complete the 'learning cycle'. Although a few managers may have a learning style that is more 'reflective' the majority are likely to begin with concrete experience. Yet much of formal learning is based on more abstract reflection and is thus of a 'knowledge-push' nature rather than being 'learning-pull'.

Later in this chapter we have some further frameworks through which strategic learning can be diagnosed. It is best, however, to start off with an anchor in your experience, as follows.

Introductory exercise

Let us begin by helping you examine your own past and recent experiences of learning to highlight whether these are 'strategic' or not.

The experiences that you choose to draw on for this exercise might be diverse. For example, it may involve the decision to allocate a particularly important project or responsibility to a specific person; or it may be how a change in the organization was handled. It could be concerned with how a sensitive issue was communicated. Possibly it might be how you responded to a piece of bad news – for instance, that a business area thought to be profitable, suddenly made a loss.

Exercise 2.1 Reflecting on recent experiences (15 minutes)

Reflecting on your business experiences over the past twelve months:

1. What experience stands out as being a major achievement (experience A)?
2. Which experience stands out as being a major trauma (experience T)?
3. For each of these two experiences (A and T), what were the key issues that had an impact on how events turned out?
4. What might you do differently in a similar situation next time?
5. What would you have done in the same way but perhaps with more vigour?
6. Following these reflections, what added insights do you feel you have now distilled from these experiences?
7. Where you have gained new insights, why were you not able to glean these at the time?
8. How do you think you may be able to extract the learning lessons from future experiences as you go?

At this point, *spend at least 15 minutes* working through this exercise. If possible, think through not just something that went well, but also something that didn't go well. Now please begin.

Some readers may have spotted that this exercise makes use of the 'critical incident technique', whereby insights are generated from past experience by examining critical incidents. Arguably, there would be no need for critical incident analysis if managers drew out the full value of learning as they make decisions, carry out activities and monitor their results. It would happen as a continuous process.

Insights that you should have gained from this exercise are as follows:

1. Where you did achieve something very successfully, it was possibly because all the *critical success factors* were aligned, and at the right time. This probably involved thinking ahead about issues that might have either a direct or an indirect impact.
2. It probably also suggested to you areas in which you have distinctive competence (or, alternatively, where it was a trauma, an area where you have a major blind spot).

A *critical success factor* is a variable that is likely to be decisive in bringing about, or frustrating, the achievement of your objective. Analysis of critical success factors is a particularly useful element in strategic learning because:

1. It forces you to stand back from effects and to examine the causal chains that bring about those effects. It therefore looks at issues *in context*.
2. It provides a means of analysing issues *before* and *after* the event. This enables you to anticipate possible events and to check, subsequently, any of your assumptions that did not hold.
3. It crystallizes these into a small number of factors that can therefore be easily communicated and provide a steer to both action and learning.

Learning from the learning process

The point of this exercise was several-fold. First, it does not come naturally to us to spend time reflecting in a systematic way. If we have secured a major achievement, then we probably rush on to the next exciting task without realizing why the achievement was a success. Alternatively, if it was a failure we would often rather not like to go back and dwell upon it.

Some learning theorists have made a big issue out of how managers and professionals find it very difficult to reflect objectively on mistakes. Argyris[2] calls these 'self-sealing errors'. Clever individuals appear (paradoxically) to be *less* inclined to admit to, let alone explore, errors. For instance, Argyris studied groups of strategy consultants and found that when a job 'went wrong' in their internal discussions they tended to push the responsibility back onto the client. They did not appear capable of reflecting on why 'errors' had actually happened, not because they were stupid but because this was simply too uncomfortable, given their culture of being 'clever'.

The same phenomenon can be observed throughout managerial life. Errors often compound, and instead of admitting to a mistake, management commitment has a habit of building rather than reducing. Sometimes the activity acquires its own momentum and appears unstoppable (for example, when companies make a determined search for acquisitions). You then have a case of 'rapidly escalating commitment'.

So not only is it often difficult for individuals to reflect on what they have learned, but it is also difficult for groups to have a genuinely open, learning style. Sometimes this can result in the dangerous condition known as 'groupthink' – a concept that goes back to the US experience in Vietnam and also, *vis-à-vis* Cuba, the 'Bay of Pigs' débâcle.

Groupthink is the phenomenon where a group of individuals' perspectives on an issue converge so that they oversimplify reality and overlook uncertainties and risks.

A personal illustration of groupthink

Some years ago I embarked on a major research project. The objective was to explore how senior management in several major companies linked corporate strategy with making major, financial decisions. My research partner and I decided to seek funding from a number of companies and enlisted the help of a major consulting firm to identify possible participants.

My research collaborator, Pete Gold, and I met two partners – Jim Trueborough and Dave Fairbank – of the major consulting firm in their offices somewhere in central London. A brief reconstruction of our thinking processes is given below. In addition to what is actually said, the reconstruction also shows what my own thoughts were at the time (these are *italicized*). This follows a process pioneered by Argyris – used to surface what is going on behind the surface of meetings.

Pete Gold: It's nice to see you again Jim, but let's get down to business. Bluntly, I think we have a very attractive research project that your clients could learn a lot through. How should we best proceed in targeting companies?

Jim Trueborough: I certainly agree, I think that we could very easily get six, no seven, possibly eight companies involved.

TG: Jim was always an optimist, will we really get as many as eight?

Dave Fairbank: Yes, it is a very exciting proposition. We are very interested ourselves in finding out more about linking strategy and finance. There are sure to be a number of our really big clients who have major problems in this area.

TG: Well yes, but exactly which clients, the finance director, the chief executive, who?

Pete Gold: So how will you target them? What can we do to help? And will you be too busy to do enough to secure our research sites if you have too much work on in the near future?

TG: Well said, Pete, they may well say one thing then do another.

Jim Trueborough: Don't worry Pete, we have all the resources to do this. I am sure that we can get a good number between us – certainly six and possibly eight. But how many will you and Tony be able to pull on board?

TG: I wondered when Jim or Dave would want to share the load?

Tony Grundy: We can have a shot at getting two, but that leaves four to six to you. By what date should we agree to have enough companies between us to go ahead?

TG: I am getting more and more concerned now – these are people who are moving at great speed. Have they really thought it through (and I haven't) or are we falling into a 'commitment trap' here?

What actually happened as a result of this case of groupthink was that just four companies agreed to participate. But this was after the consulting firm had become very busy and several months had passed without result. Also, only two of the four research participants came via this channel. Indeed, it proved very difficult to get companies to sign up to the research – because (one suspects) of embarrassment of revealing difficulties in strategic decision-making to outsiders.

With hindsight this was just as well, as we had more than enough to cope with in analysing four research sites. Six would have been very, very stretching and eight . . . impossible! Yet we all felt (after what seemed to be an intelligent debate) that all the angles were well covered.

Not all instances of groupthink are as recoverable as this one was, however. There are many cases where this has led to major disasters – for example, through ill-thought-out senior appointments (the celebrated MD brought in from outside who doesn't 'fit in' and leaves within two years), acquisition and diversification programmes, restructuring programmes which appear to oscillate between centralization and decentralization.

The key lessons here are that apparent *levels* of intelligence or training do not provide both necessary *and sufficient* conditions for sustaining strategic learning in groups. In some instances the perception that 'we are all good at analysing complex problems' can inhibit thorough reflection and testing of ideas. In addition to intelligence and training you also need to have a process for surfacing issues and assumptions, for reshaping possible decisions and for targeting activities. You must also *apply* this process rigorously and vigorously.

Exercise 2.2   Identifying groupthink (5 minutes)

From experiences over your management career:

1. What examples of groupthink can you identify?
2. What were the factors that led to this phenomenon occurring (for example, business and organizational pressures and temptations; the role and influence of specific individuals; the mind-set of the group of managers; the dynamics of decision-making)?
3. What were the consequences of groupthink in this case?
4. Did the managers involved actually *learn* from the experience?

This will not be, by far, the last time you encounter groupthink. You will face this many times in the coming months, but will you now be able to recognize it? And will you be prepared to challenge it, rather than go along with it through drift?

These are the kind of key questions that need to be faced if strategic learning is to be effective.

Following this analysis of groupthink, let us now consider in Sections 2.3–2.5 how the process of strategic learning can be created and sustained.

2.3   The pathways and perils of organizational learning

So far we have dealt principally with learning at the individual level. It is now time to explore the issues faced in spreading learning through the wider organization.

You will achieve this by first looking at different schools of thought of organizational learning. We then consider some practical examples of complex learning before turning back to these schools of thought.

The differing schools of thought include:

1. The *prescriptive* school, which believes that organizations must learn in order to survive and to thrive. They should strive to become genuine 'learning organizations'.
2. The *impossibility* school, which believes that attempts to spread learning throughout any complex organization will founder upon a number of obstacles – for instance, denial of error, avoidance of uncertainty and ambiguity, or pure business politics.
3. The *pragmatic* school, which believes that although there are many barriers to strategic learning, islands or pools of learning can be created within an organization. These islands need a lot of effort if learning is to be developed and sustained. However, with continual effort, learning routines become built in to 'how we do things around here' and may ultimately reach a critical mass to form joined-up, learning continents.

Later in this chapter we put the argument for the 'pragmatic school', but for the moment let us (briefly) explore each school in turn.

The prescriptive school has many proponents: Senge[3] in the US, among many others (for instance, Garratt[4] in the UK, and, in a much more moderated form, by Pedler *et al.*[5] Further, writers like to see learning in terms of challenge, or contention – for example, Tom Peters' *Thriving on Chaos*[6] and, more recently, Pascale's *Managing on the Edge.*[7] While highlighting the need to foster learning throughout complex organizations, they leave the practitioner wondering 'How do I begin?' and 'How difficult or impossible is this Herculean task?'.

However, the problem with these prescriptive ideals is that managers may be unable or unwilling to lead by example in changing their style. Without appropriate support and without mobilization as teams of 'open thinkers' individual action is very likely to be frustrated.

The impossibility school, by contrast, suggests that complex forms of (strategic) learning are highly unstable and are very difficult to share and sustain within an organization. Argyris[2] argues that most managers are comfortable with simpler forms of learning, where the task around which the learning centres is repeated essentially in the same form or the same loop ('single-loop' learning).

However, managers are much less comfortable with more open and unpredictable learning. Argyris describes this as 'double-loop' learning to suggest that managers are learning to do *new* tasks effectively, and often old tasks in *new* ways.

Single-loop learning would tend to take a problem as more or less as given, and as discrete and well defined. Double-loop learning involves a considerably wider exploration of the problem. The problem may thus be redefined and will be looked at from a number of perspectives. Because of the range of choices in exploring this kind of issue there is a much higher chance of error than with single-loop learning.

To strengthen his argument, Argyris highlights an important dilemma: many managers and professionals are highly competent at doing the more routine and technical tasks. However, they are often less competent at dealing with more open-ended, uncertain and ambiguous issues. In particular, they may oversimplify the problem. They may be very prone to oversimplification when alternative, wider definitions of the problem, either by others within their team or by outsiders, may imply error on their part. Argyris graphically highlights this often chronic aversion to exposing error in his case studies. Let us now explore a more recent case at length to illustrate the differences between single- and double-loop learning.

A case of single- versus double-loop learning

A dozen senior managers from a financial services company, Uranus Investments, were involved in a 'strategic implementation' programme. The goals of this modular programme were:

- to develop their capacity to think strategically
- to apply this approach to how they manage operationally
- to simulate both strategic thinking and action in two business development projects.

Before the programme, the in-house human resources manager applied psychometric tests to find out more about the mix of their management and learning styles. The results indicated that there were only a few of the managers with a more innovative bent, and most were highly action oriented.

The learning programme was structured in three phases:

1. A three-day workshop was conducted so that Uranus' managers could become acquainted with key strategic concepts and learn how to manage implementation strategically.
2. Data were collected for the business development project, back in the organization.
3. A five-day session was conducted off-site to analyse project data and to create and evaluate options to be presented to Board members.

Although attempts were made prior to the programme to set expectations about the programme's different focus and style from managers' previous experiences, this message had not been understood. As the facilitator arrived at the luxurious hotel in the Cotswolds and sought to unload materials at the rear of the tropical swimming pool, he was being surreptitiously observed. Apparently programme members who thought they had been invited to a few days' course in pleasant circumstances became nervous at the scale of preparations. This looked like hard work!

Despite a clear statement at the beginning of the programme that it would involve a lot of lateral thinking, with few exceptions it was clear that the message had not been fully assimilated. By the second day participants appeared to be getting jumpy and uncomfortable. One group in particular had great trouble brainstorming ideas for the business development project, despite intensive facilitation.

Late on Day 2, the facilitator decided that it was opportune to reflect on their learning experiences, as follows:

> It seems that you have been struggling to move out of your normal way of thinking and learning. What we have been doing [writing on the flip chart, see Table 2.1] is dealing with a much messier pattern of ideas than your normal job accustoms you to. You need to be more patient in exploring the issues, while using the strategic tools and frameworks to give you focus and direction.

Table 2.1 Operational vs strategic thinking and learning

Operational thinking and learning	Strategic thinking and learning
Programmed and deductive	Open, creative and intuitive
Clear boundaries and structures	Ambiguous and ill-structured
Assumptions are given	Surfacing and questioning of assumptions
Linear and predictable process	Fluid and interactive process
'Hard' outputs – detailed but determinate	'Hard' and soft outputs – patterns and hard insights
Low uncertainty and fear	High uncertainty, fear and defensiveness

The managers visibly relaxed when this picture (which distinguished operational action and thinking from strategic learning) was fed back to them. This became a turning point for the programme. Subsequently both groups went on to produce projects which genuinely impressed the Uranus Board members by their depth of thinking and insight.

During the programme, the individual styles of managers had made it much more difficult to jump learning tracks from single to double loop. At one stage one of the groups looked so depressed that to lighten their mood the facilitator suggested: 'Well, don't worry [turning to the window and opening it], I see we are on the second floor – who wants to jump out first?'

This joke broke the seriousness of the group – double-loop learning doesn't have to be very serious or gloomy, on the contrary it may need to be lightened. Strategic learning is very difficult when individuals or the group as a whole are all tense.

This incident also highlights that not only is it difficult to jump learning tracks from single to double loop, but it is also worrying and potentially frightening.

The key lessons from this case are:

1. Where managers are deeply ingrained in their single-loop, routine learning tracks, it is difficult to get them to jump on to a more uncertain, complex and possibly threatening learning track.
2. Managers need to have a mix of support but firm guidance. (In this case example, another breakthrough occurred when the facilitator appeared to lose patience and said, 'You really must let go of the old ways of looking at things'. Subsequently it turned out that this helped them see the facilitator as 'one of us' and not just another 'human resources type' (these were their words and not the facilitator's).)
3. If there are a number of tools and frameworks with which managers are unfamiliar, or where the focus of learning is beyond their more recent experience, they need considerably more time to gain a sound learning platform.
4. Sometimes it may be better to give participants the control over whether a presentation of outputs should be made to senior management rather than to pre-schedule this. If they feel more in control of whether to present, or what and when to present, then this removes undue uncertainty and diminishes fear.
5. Although double-loop learning is difficult (and more difficult for some than for others) it is possible to orchestrate it with managers working in learning groups. The problem, however, is how to *sustain* the learning once the learning group is disbanded.

We return later to how double-loop learning can be sustained, particularly in the cases on Dowty (Chapter 5) and Mercury Communications (Chapter 6). Let us now come back, however, to address the different schools of organizational learning.

The earlier case highlights how difficult it may be in some organizations to become much more fluid or to introduce open learning systems. Even where a learning setting is created deliberately there are many forces inhibiting learning. This is compounded by the many barriers and boundaries built into organizational architecture. If it is difficult to open up *individuals* and *groups* to more complex learning, then surely it will be impossible to do this at an organizational level?

This conclusion does not, however, follow. One of the main barriers to freeing up the learning in the earlier case was its very narrow focus on a very small percentage of managers in the organization. It was also conducted in a fairly narrow time frame of two months. Whatever shift in learning style might have been induced in this tiny minority it is likely to have been rapidly neutralized by wider organizational forces. This is akin to a kind of 'learning sandcastle', which looked robust until a few waves of the tide lapped it away.

While one might be sympathetic to the idea of, and need for, 'learning organizations', this seems to be a very distant vision for most, if not all, companies. Although it is a useful idea, it may perhaps be more effective to work towards this goal on a more pragmatic basis. While attempts to create tiny and isolated pockets of learning (as in the financial services case) should be avoided, there are many opportunities to move forward by creating and developing a network of islands of strategic learning. This can be accomplished through the pragmatic approach which I now advocate as a means of achieving strategic learning in practice.

The pragmatic approach thus:

- seeks to build a critical mass of learning through intensive involvement in group work and distributes the learning through organizational feedback, steering existing initiatives and setting up new ones as an ongoing process;
- avoids attempts to build learning islands which are small, isolated and positioned purely or primarily as training activities;
- exploits existing approaches to, for instance, quality management, project management, empowerment, rather than being seen as a separate initiative, thus making strategic learning the glue that binds management processes and initiatives together;
- targets to achieve early and major business and organizational benefits.

The pragmatic approach is illustrated in each of the cases in this book. Before we leave the topic of pathways and perils of organizational learning, it is opportune to offer you an important checklist – one that you should pin to the wall.

CHECKLIST OF MUST DO'S AND NEVER DO'S IN
STRATEGIC LEARNING

Must Do's

1. Always *position* the process effectively.
2. Always set *expectations* and reinforce them.
3. Always *target* for some specific business and organizational benefits.
4. Always provide *learning frameworks* that are *simple* but *powerful* to steer the analysis.
5. Always ensure that the learning process is effectively *facilitated*.

Never Do's

1. Never restrict *involvement* to one level or functional area of management.
2. Never restrict *time* and *resources* unduly.
3. Never *seal up* the process so that it is seen as a discrete exercise, for example as a training programme, one away day or merely as a one-off planning exercise.
4. Never *fuzz* outputs and their implications in order to make them acceptable and to preserve comfort levels – thereby softening their challenge unduly.
5. Never fail to manage *stakeholders* effectively.

2.4   A framework for strategic learning

Bringing reality into learning

With one or two notable exceptions, the theme of 'learning' was not at the top of the management agenda until fairly recently – either in practice or in academia. In practical circles, with the exception of action learning,[8] learning was associated with training, and training was seen as primarily an off-line activity.

When managers already hold senior positions a high learning capability is often assumed, irrespective of the formal development they have undergone or the series of roles they have been involved in, or their balance of experience. Equally, group learning is more often regarded purely as interaction or 'team-building'. Organizational learning is either considered to be subsumed within culture change or similar initiatives, or it has a narrow, high-level channel via strategic planning. Most organizations approach learning in a highly fragmented way. Learning needs are typically seen to be the same as training and development needs, rather than – as perhaps they ought to be – a fundamental means of achieving competitive advantage.

To summarize, what the notion of 'strategic learning' therefore does is to help dissolve compartmentalized thinking about learning. At the same time it involves being pragmatic and realistic in tackling the barriers to viewing learning as a core management process.

Mastering the learning cycle

The above issues suggest a more intricate learning cycle than that proposed by Kolb,[1] which appears more suited to simpler, or single-loop learning. A useful framework was arrived at as a result of research on strategic learning of senior managers conducted at Cranfield,[9] as shown in Figure 2.1. This highlights some form of learning stimulus being followed by experimentation, then filtering against past perspectives. Finally, there is a process of reflection which may result in some change in perspectives.

Kolb's learning theory tends to focus primarily on *individual* rather than *group* learning. Group learning, which is a more natural forum for strategic learning, involves not merely a learning stimulus but also a learning vehicle of some kind. This learning vehicle might take the form of a single meeting or a series of meetings. It may extend to a more substantive project, workshop, or a wider or longer programme in the organization.

Subsequent to experimentation we also see filtering as an important stage within the learning process. Here, experiences are interpreted relative to past concepts, experiences and feelings. Some of these may be peculiar to individuals, whereas others will be shared. Organizational theory is awash with ideas for dealing with the filtering process, including 'constructs',

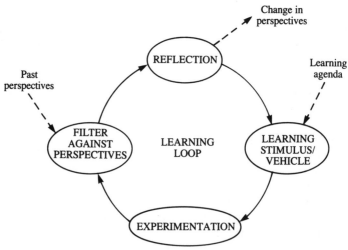

Figure 2.1   Understanding strategic learning

'schema', 'frames of reference', 'mindsets' and finally 'perspectives' – the latter being a term that is perhaps closest to everyday speech.

The second loop is called the 'action loop' (Figure 2.2) as it begins with matching experience to need. This takes the learner(s) back to the driving agendas which motivate action. Where individuals are learning as part of a group process their agendas will be multiple and overlapping, which explains why facilitation is of paramount importance not merely to move forward but to define the agenda. The dual-loop structure of learning has some resemblance to Garratt's 'policy' and 'operations' loops.[4]

Following this there is an additional phase of a more detailed needs assessment to identify areas for possible experimentation. At this stage, from my research at Cranfield, managers appear intuitively to relate needs to the perceived gap between where they are now and where they wish to be (or feel they ought to be).

A further important stage is that of amplifying the need. This is important as experimentation will involve effort, and possibly some risk. It may also be in competition with other areas of opportunity for action. Often learning is viewed as an imperative by proponents of management learning – a good thing in itself, but in reality managers have so many competing claims on their time that competitive rivalry for their attention is intense and acute.[10] Therefore a critical success factor for strategic learning is that the perceived

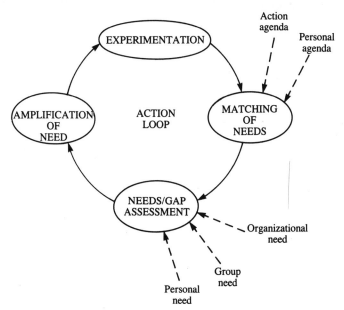

Figure 2.2   Understanding strategic action

need to experiment *increases*. A second critical success factor is the ability to deal with *distractions*, which can be legion. These phenomena are graphically shown in the illustrations presented later in this chapter.

Figure 2.3 integrates the learning and action loops so that we see strategic learning as a dual system of action and learning. Within organizations both loops are in operation simultaneously, but are often not well synchronized. In some instances they may work against each other – for instance, where learning insights occur but are not strong enough to challenge the major activities to which the organization is already deeply committed.

An important feature in Figure 2.3 is that of distraction. In many instances there may be such a degree of competition for managers' attention that instead of reinforcement (amplification of need), the issues or insights are lost or lie unutilized as a result of distraction. This may be far from being the exception – much of the learning achieved in strategic workshops can be

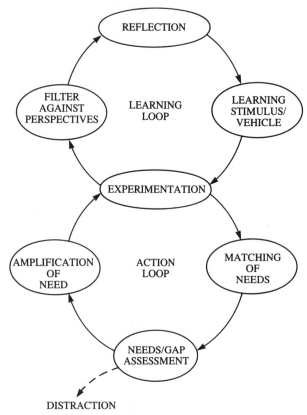

Figure 2.3   Linking strategic learning and action (1)

lost as the awareness of the problem rapidly folds back on itself once it has opened up.

The above suggests an important idea: that of the *learning window of opportunity*. Unless learning is quickly capitalized on it rapidly becomes overlaid and may disintegrate owing to other issues and activities. This is not to say that it has ceased to exist. In archaeological terms it may still be possible to find it, or to excavate it, but it has often become so buried that its effect is neutral.

Finally, in the strategic learning process, Figure 2.4 highlights a number of areas where the loops of learning can be facilitated. For instance:

- *for reflection*: formal, strategic analysis and evaluation frameworks for reflection and filtering
- *for the learning stimulus*: strategic workshops, projects and reviews to act as learning stimuli and vehicles
- *for experimentation*: implementation frameworks[11] for moving round or reducing barriers to change
- *for matching of needs*: strategic measures and controls to assess how possible action is matched to need
- *for needs/gap analysis*: strategic positioning – understanding where you are now against where you want to be (visioning) helps to assess needs and the gap between existing and desired states.

In the second and third parts of this book we explore the advantages and disadvantages of particular ways of intervening to generate strategic learning in action.

In addition, there may be powerful strategic recipes[12] which guide strategic thinking and decision-making in the organization. These 'recipes' or rules of thumb may prescribe certain types of activity, or may prohibit them. The recipes can be shared by the organization or may be introduced by specific individuals, for instance by a new chief executive hired from the outside.

Moving back now to the learning process, it is best to illustrate some of the key ingredients of the double-loop cycle (Figure 2.4). This is illustrated using a few examples from my research at Cranfield.

Strategic learning across four major companies

This research was conducted with eight senior managers in strategic learning workshops, with two participants coming from each of the four companies. The four companies included International Distillers and Vintners (IDV, a

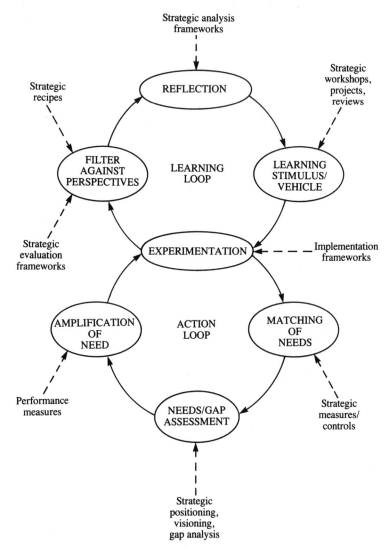

Figure 2.4 Software for strategic learning

major division of GrandMet), London Underground, Rolls-Royce Aero-engines, and finally Post Office Counters.

The eight managers met for nearly four days in two sessions to explore issues associated with making strategic investment decisions. They were invited to learn from each other's experiences across the four companies and also from existing theory and frameworks on how strategic investment decisions are made. They were also invited to challenge existing management theory on this problem.

Between one workshop and the next there was opportunity for managers to experiment on live issues. Participants were tracked to see the extent to which they implemented changes in decision-making as a result of the learning exercise (as depicted in Figure 2.5).

During the workshops there were some clear instances of learning breakthroughs; for instance, a Rolls-Royce manager said:

> Having talked (these issues) around this group of (cross-organization) managers, it certainly brought it home to me. It is fundamental to try to define the new base case (where we do nothing) *before* deciding what the value of the strategic investment will be.

The above example highlights a shift in this manager's perspectives in how he understands the strategic and financial analysis of a major investment decision. The 'base case' of the business (i.e. what happens to it without the

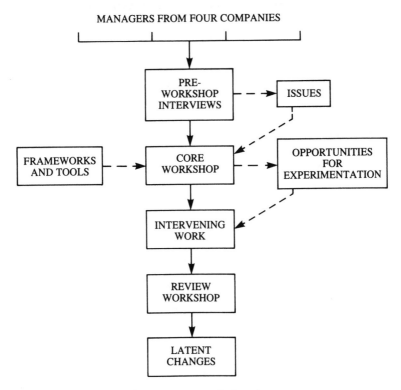

Figure 2.5   An action research process: strategic learning

investment) does *not* mean that nothing happens and everything remains exactly as previously.

There were many other examples where managers moved beyond reflection (and subsequent change in perspectives) to more concrete experimentation. For instance, the same Rolls-Royce manager said:

> You have the problem of communicating the trade-off (to the Board) between short-term value and long-term value. And I found it quite helpful, seeing whether the share price stacked up against the value of the projects. I did a sort of crude grid, *I don't know who gave me the idea.*

> I just plotted the present values over five years on the vertical axis and the rest of the present value over the life on the horizontal. It was quite a convenient shorthand way of marrying our corporate plan with the underlying value of the strategy. If it doesn't (all match up) then we've got a problem, someone else can come in and pay more for it.

This episode illustrates how the manager made up his own way of analysing the value of the corporate strategy. Thus frameworks were filtered in order to be assimilated. Also, there was a matching of needs which related back to his perceived learning gap – of how senior management could bridge strategic vision with financial planning. More importantly, the 'amplification of need' came from the Board's interest in maximizing shareholder value. The experimentation in the use of strategic concepts was facilitated by a number of factors which had become aligned in both the learning and action loops.

In one of the other companies an important insight was gained but then decayed – that the company should set *explicit* (rather than implicit) strategic objectives for its investment programme and projects. At the time, both managers from the company became excited with this insight, and apparently very determined to experiment with the concept:

> I think in our submissions we ought to say this project is about cost savings, and this project is about improved customer perception.

After the workshop, his enthusiasm appeared to waiver:

> We're interested in it (strategic objectives) in theory, but is it actually, are there other similar organizations doing it, is it a positive weakness that we aren't doing it, or is it just something which is pretty?

By the second workshop (six months later) the same manager suddenly remembered:

> I remember it, but we haven't actually followed it through in detail ... we wanted to do it and we didn't.

It would appear that there had been little internal amplification here encouraging experimentation. Contrast this with another example which led on to successful experimentation for the same managers:

> It is worth mentioning that we used graphics a lot more this year. The interesting thing was, we went on to sell this to our external shareholders. They could see the areas of colour (what we were spending and why). It is an interesting concept because selling a programme on what you see rather than on what you add up is not the way we have worked before.

Again, this innovation appears to be linked to some of the learning stimulus/frameworks that depicted investment programmes in pictorial, as opposed to numerical, terms. But the managers had drawn from this idea and had applied it their own way – and with the reinforcement and amplification of interest from their managing directors.

During this study, a very large number of complex issues surfaced (over 50 in fact), most of which were then reflected on in depth by the eight managers. However, in only a smaller number of cases did this result in a significant shift in managers' perspectives, and in an even smaller number did this translate through to experimentation.

The above result highlights the selectiveness of the filtering process and also the sifting of needs and the need for reinforcement and amplification of insights. It also highlights the need for very well-targeted learning indeed.

Although strategic learning can thus generate a considerable volume of rich ideas it is often just a handful, however, that can be extremely powerful. For instance, a few of the insights and techniques created by managers at Rolls-Royce Aeroengines were subsequently used in the appraisal of some very major corporate decisions. Also at Post Office Counters managers subsequently did a lot of work to flesh out the business strategy and make much closer links with financial appraisal than previously.

It is now useful to bring in the earlier framework in Chapter 1 of SARTRE – surfacing, analysing, reshaping, targeting, resolving and experimenting – see Figure 2.6. This shows the surfacing and analysing elements to be closely integrated with the 'learning loop'. It also links reshaping to matching of needs, and targeting to needs assessment, and moves towards resolving key issues. Resolving key issues follows on from amplification of need.

Learning versus unlearning

Even with well-focused learning a good deal of important insights may thus be lost or decay, resulting in an *unlearning curve*. However, the fact that experimentation does not necessarily occur immediately does not mean that

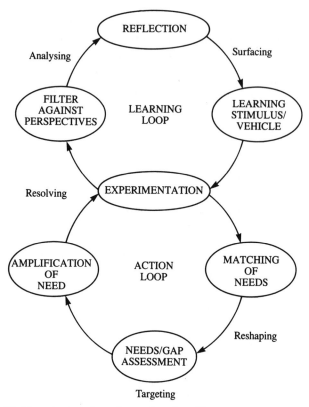

Figure 2.6 Linking strategic learning and action (2)

it will *never* occur. For instance, in one of the Cranfield cases relatively few instances of concrete experimentation were noted during the field research (a one-year period). However, subsequently one of the managers went on to champion an important project on competitor analysis.

The above examples of strategic learning suggest that learning may occur but may then suffer a variety of fates. This depends upon the perceived utility and novelty of insights.

Figure 2.7 explores some of these possibilities by plotting the novelty of an insight against its perceived utility. This picture helps us explain why some learning dissipates while other learning seems to go into suspended animation.

While, by Figure 2.7, novelty of insight (relative to existing perspectives) should require no amplification, the perceived utility may be the result of two factors: the importance of the issue (I) and the probability of having to deal with it (P). Perceived utility can be expressed, therefore, as $(I) \times (P)$.

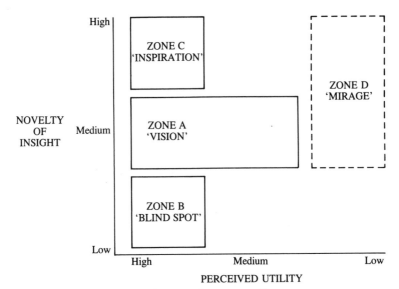

Figure 2.7 Capturing the learning: novelty versus utility

Figure 2.7 highlights a range of possibilities. For instance, Zone A ('Vision') highlights areas of learning with medium novelty and with medium to high perceived utility. Zone A is where most of the experimentation will occur in many organizations (other than in the most innovative). Although other insights may have higher novelty, these may also result in greater discomfort in managers putting these into action (unless the perceived utility is very high indeed – see Zone C, 'Inspiration').

Zone B ('Blind spot') is likely to result in more experimentation than Zone C ('Inspiration') even though insights are less novel. Here there is even more chance of active experimentation because Zone B is perceived as less threatening (unless the insights are trivial).

Yet the above analysis flies in the face of how many learning initiatives are set up. Often they are positioned as 'new' or 'leading edge' (across the top of Figure 2.7) with the result that what ensues is a 'pure learning experience'.

Figure 2.7 also highlights that some areas may provoke significant insights but be seen (at the time) as being of low perceived utility (Zone D, 'Mirage'). This may be because of the perceived low probability of having to deal with them, even though they are important through having potentially high impact. Yet events may shift Zone D to the left for managers, suddenly crystallizing in experimentation many months and possibly a year or more later.

Individual managers may also differ considerably as to how much patience they have for storing up insights in Zone D. This may also vary at different stages of their careers. As they mature, they may become more open to broadening their perspectives in case they need to meet unexpected issues – or equally, they may narrow their interest. This suggests that managers go through varying cycles of *openness to learning* in their careers.

The learning and related action loops are dynamic over time. They may be kick-started after any observer has left the scene. This makes it particularly difficult to assess the value of strategic learning – at least precisely and accurately. But, as has been argued elsewhere,[6] intangibles may have financial value even though this value cannot be measured precisely.

Integrating learning, action and capability

How do the learning and action loops link to wider systems or loops within the organization? Two important areas that are linked into this are those of strategic vision and of organizational capability.

Figure 2.8 shows how strategic vision and organizational capability fit

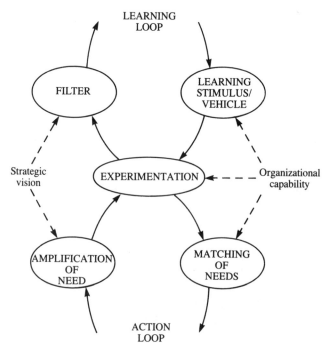

Figure 2.8 Bringing in strategic vision and capability

into strategic learning. Strategic vision is thus important as a way of guiding the filtering process. Where the vision is weak or not well communicated, this may make it very difficult for managers to move forward.

One London Underground manager reflects that:

> If this is going to be our strategy it (pricing policy) will be this, if that is going to be our strategy it will be that ... strategic double vision, and this week we seem to be somewhere in the middle.

These impressions of the *strategic ambiguity* that clouds many organizations are not isolated. Another piece of research at Cranfield[13] revealed that within a particular management team individuals may often have very different views indeed of what their business competitive strategy is and how this is changing.

We return to the debate about whether, and to what extent, strategy should be fluid or ambiguous later in our discussions of styles of strategic management in Chapter 3. Suffice it to say that strategic ambiguity in an organization can greatly impede the clarity of decision-making. This was especially evident in the Uranus Investments case, continued from earlier.

Brief flashback to the Uranus Investments case

In the Business Development Programme described earlier the learning focus was a specific problem set by a Board director. A question was set which asked how the Group could extend its business scope through profitable development – and achieve this at low risk, or at lower levels than those of core operations. During the project the director visited the project teams to present how the project fitted in with overall strategy for the Group. Unfortunately this had the opposite effect of what was originally intended. Instead of clarifying the strategic direction it generated more confusion and ambiguity for the managers. This was because the 'strategy' seemed to be broad. It was based on targeted financial results and market trends, missing out key aspects of competitive position and capability.

Another important and wider issue that emerged from the exercise was that of the need to improve organizational capability. The level of capability impacts on the kind of learning that will be most effective or indeed *possible*. For instance, where an organization already practises cross-functional project management or quality management initiatives, this may provide ready vehicles for strategic learning. Alternatively, where managers deal with 90 per cent of issues through meetings or committees, this will no doubt impair the organization's capacity for strategic learning.

Gaps in capability may also have a bearing on the kind of needs that are prioritized as being important. A capability gap may suggest that action is *more* important or urgent than improving capability *per se*. However, the existence of this gap may diminish motivation to act as it is perceived as 'mission impossible'. Ideally, strategic learning should seek to achieve a double-hit – mobilizing some area of action *and* also building capability.

Strategic learning has therefore been found to have the following qualities:

1. It is considerably more involved than some of the more evangelical proponents of the learning organization appear to suggest. There are very many things to get right to make it effective.
2. It is able, however, to deliver some major organizational insights and benefits – the fruits of strategic learning are worth the effort.
3. It requires sustained and timely effort to amplify insights and needs: this is necessary to seize and lengthen the 'learning window of opportunity' and to avoid a steep unlearning curve (for unlearning, see Hedberg[14]).
4. It recognizes that managers naturally focus on areas of highest immediate utility. Their thinking then needs to be stretched to cover areas of possible utility for the future.

2.5 Concluding lessons

Strategic learning is a complex but potentially powerful process that may yield great advantage for the organization. However, to create, sustain and to harvest the full value of strategic learning requires considerable effort and skill. None the less, you may have achieved some significant insights merely in doing the short exercises in this chapter, which underlines the fact that there are always some benefits.

Without sufficient effort and skill, however, strategic learning is unlikely to be sustained. It is more likely to result in strategic *unlearning*, as the Cranfield study graphically illustrated. The more complex the learning, the more rapid the decay of insights is likely to be.

Also, as strategic learning is complex, fluid and not easy to share and disseminate, it may sometimes have a relatively short 'half-life', especially if it is not well supported or amplified. This emphasizes the need for quick translation of learning into decisions and action.

In the next chapter we shall take a closer look at the quest for competitive advantage at the business level, and how strategic learning can contribute to it.

References

1. Kolb, D. A., *Experiential Learning*, Prentice-Hall, New Jersey, 1984.
2. Argyris, C., 1991, 'Teaching smart people how to learn', *Harvard Business Review*, May–June, 1991, pp. 99–109.
3. Senge, P., *The Fifth Discipline: The Art and Practice of the Learning Organisation*, Century Business, 1990.
4. Garratt, B., *Creating a Learning Organisation*, Director Books, Cambridge, 1990.
5. Pedler, M., Burgoyne, J. and Boydell, T., *The Learning Company*, McGraw-Hill, 1991.
6. Peters, T., *Thriving on Chaos*, Macmillan, 1987.
7. Pascale, R. T., *Managing on the Edge*, Penguin, 1990.
8. Revans, R. W., *Action Learning, New Techniques for Management*, Bland and Briggs, 1980.
9. Grundy, A. N., *Corporate Strategy and Financial Decisions*, Kogan Page, 1992.
10. Porter, M. E., *Competitive Advantage*, The Free Press, New York, 1985.
11. Grundy, A. N., *Implementing Strategic Change*, Kogan Page, 1993.
12. Spender, J. C., 'Strategy making in business', PhD Thesis, School of Business, University of Manchester, 1980.
13. Bowman, C., 'Interpreting competitive strategy', in *The Challenge of Strategic Management* (ed. D. F. Faulkner and G. Johnson), Kogan Page, 1992.
14. Hedberg. B.,'How organisations learn and unlearn', in *Handbook of Organisational Design*, Vol. 1 (ed. D. Nystrom and W. Starbuck), Oxford University Press, 1981, pp. 3–27.

3
Learning and dynamic competitive advantage

3.1 What is competitive advantage?

This chapter deals with how learning can help create dynamic competitive advantage for your business. This brings strategic learning directly on to the agenda of top management, which is an important plank of positioning strategic learning as a key management process.

We begin by looking at different notions of competitive advantage and suggest a practical route forward for managers in building reinforcing sources of advantage. The argument is put that competitive advantage must be understood dynamically – over time – and that strategic learning can help create and sustain that advantage. This involves exploring four key phases of exploiting strategic learning.

Finally we consider the impact of internal dynamics: we explore how change within the organization creates competitive advantage and how it can be managed through strategic learning. Let us first define competitive advantage:

> *Competitive advantage is how a business competes so that it generates **more value** for its customers than its key competitors, or generates similar value at **less cost** or in **less time**.*

This definition is based on ideas very close to those of Ohmae[1] and Porter.[2] In addition, the notion of time was also included to emphasize the dynamic quality of competitive advantage.

3.2 Why is static advantage not enough?

Before examining competitive advantage more closely, let us first consider the concept of strategy. The idea of strategy is important because it brings together a single view of the advantages of an organization. It achieves this by relating the organization to its present and future environment and also to the aspirations of its key stakeholders.

What is strategy?

Many fortunes have been made by writers of strategic management in extolling the virtues of corporate planning, corporate strategy, competitive strategy and also of competitive advantage. Unfortunately ideas of 'strategy' appear to be stretched and distorted by managers. This may be deliberate, by inexperience or accident.

Strategy has often received a mixed reception by managers who are cynical as a result of the many abuses that have beset the idea. The following examples give some typical abuses of the notion of strategy, with the real meanings in italics:

'We are stripping back to our core business.' [*We are forced to divest of poorly related and understood acquisitions which cost us money and pushed up our borrowing.*]

'The acquisition of new distribution channels will generate new synergies for the Group.' [*We shall urgently be rationalizing operations and cutting costs.*]

'The business case contains a strategic opportunity with major upsides.' [*We are unable to quantify or qualify the scale of the opportunity, the structure of the emerging industry and competitive rivalry, our position within it, and likely financial returns.*]

The abuse of strategy thus appears to be a classic case of 'management by ornaments' – a latter-day version of 'MBO' where managers clutter their organizations with management concepts and fashions without using them effectively. This clutter may give them a comfortable illusion that they are managing effectively when the truth could not be further away.

Strategy in practice, therefore, often contrasts sharply with strategy as prescribed by gurus. If one looks at much of the strategy literature you need not look far to find exceedingly clear views on how to design your strategy. For instance, you might ask the following ten questions, which distil this considerable literature into a tiny volume:

THE TEN-QUESTION GUIDE FOR STRATEGY DESIGN

1. What key changes are affecting or might affect your organization's competitive and wider environment?

2. What is/are the organization's business(es), and with what focus?
3. What is the organization's position relative to key competitors and possible entrants?
4. What is the organization's internal capability?
5. What new areas of business might be developed and what existing business areas should be run down or divested to restore competitive advantage?
6. How should the organization compete to gain an advantage that is genuinely *sustainable*?
7. What is the probable financial value of key strategic options, and how will financial constraints be managed?
8. How should the organization implement new development and change?
9. What resources are needed and how and when will these be procured to support competitive advantage?
10. What key milestones and controls should be used to monitor progress and competitive position?

The succinct nature of the above checklist obscures the amount of thinking and learning required to deliver a workable business strategy. For instance, at Dowty's IT Division it was estimated that the strategy for a £120m turnover, complex business took approximately 6000 hours to formulate. This strategy needed to deal with:

— a dozen countries
— ten major product/service areas
— two technology areas
— three types of distribution channel.

Where a business is relatively complex it will not suffice to do a broad-brush strategy as the competitive battlefield is highly variable, depending on which specific business area is being addressed. The strategic analysis needs to be done for *each* and *every* business area as the market segments and competitors differ.

Highly complex businesses put heavy demands upon managers' capacity for strategic learning. Equally, this may suggest that the business has become so complex that value is in effect destroyed because critical size is reached in so few areas. Where the strategic building blocks are small and differ considerably from each other, competitive advantage will be very elusive.

Perceptions of external position may also change rapidly, adding to the problem of keeping strategic vision up to date.

Case study 3.1 Venus Petrochem

The strategic planning director of Venus Petrochem (with turnover in excess of £1 billion) reflected that:

'Yes, we do use portfolio positioning grids to analyse the (a) market characteristics such as growth, margin potential, etc. and (b) measures of our own competitive position, for example market share, perceptions by our customers, etc. It is quite surprising, we look at these positionings over eighty grids every three months. In many cases there is a small shift each quarter. In six months we often see some quite major shifts. The whole process focuses managers' minds wonderfully. *It gets them to ask a lot more strategic questions, rather than just focusing on day-to-day issues.*'

What types of strategy exist?

Competitive advantage is at the cornerstone of successful business strategy. Without it, strategy may become purely visionary, or merely a set of incremental decisions that exploit a random stream of opportunities facing the organization.

There has been a considerable, and at times heated, debate over whether strategy should be set deliberately and by well-thought-out design by management (the 'design school' in its most complete form, see Porter.[2,3] *The rational* approach to strategy has been attacked, particularly by Quinn[4] who argued that strategic decisions crystallize incrementally. Although there may be some logic to this, it is very much piecemeal.

Most actual strategic decision-making in organizations appears to be mainly a product of incrementalism. But to say, therefore, that the incrementalist school is 'right' is similar to suggesting that because most cars in the UK are driven on the motorway at 75–80 mph, the 70 mph speed limit is 'wrong'.

A major attack on the design school of strategy has been made by Mintzberg,[5] who suggested the idea of 'emergent strategies'. Mintzberg argues that, in most cases, strategy cannot be decided until *after* the event: it emerges as a 'pattern in a stream of decisions'.

Exercise 3.1

Does the business strategy of your organization appear to be more akin to an *emergent* strategy that crystallizes through an incremental series of decision ('type E') or does it appear more akin to a *coherent* view of how the company competes and can continue to compete across the business it is in ('type C')? If it is more of an emergent or incremental strategy ('type E'), what are the disadvantages of this in terms of hampering clarity of decision-making? If it is more of a deliberate, well articulated strategy ('type C'), are there major disadvantages in terms of inflexibility?

This debate is not purely academic, as it has major implications for the importance of the idea of competitive advantage. It also has implications for the extent to which strategy-making and implementation are learning processes, and, if so, what kind of learning processes do they entail? Are the processes closely guided or very loose and fluid?

The argument that deliberate or coherent strategies become rapidly outdated by external change is acceptable only to the extent that 'strategy' is considered to be long term. But the 'long term' varies, depending upon the nature of the business. Even where the future becomes highly uncertain within three to five years (or less), there is still a major (if not more) need for a sense of medium-term direction.

Returning to our ten questions on strategy design, the notion of competitive advantage was often implied: question 3 (external position relative to competitors), question 4 (internal capability), question 5 (business development and retrenchment), question 6 (sustainable advantage), question 9 (access to resources) and question 10 (monitoring of advantage). This highlights how crucial competitive advantage is to securing a successful strategy.

The notion of competitive advantage itself is essentially simple. In many ways it is easier to grasp than the more lofty idea of 'strategy', which has an aura of being high level and purely longer term. This has important implications: if 'competitive advantage' becomes central within the mindset of managers at all levels, then many of the problems of making 'deliberate' strategies should dissolve.

The main barrier to achieving this breakthrough lies not so much in planning processes *per se*, but in the ability of the organization to use strategic learning to think about the impact of business issues on competitive advantage.

The dilemma between design versus emergent/incremental strategies thus appears to reflect a battle between prescriptive views. The core ideas of competitive strategy normally associated with the 'design school' are malleable. They can be disseminated easily within a complex organization – provided that the leadership allows this to happen and gives the right kind of facilitation, as we shall see later, particularly in Chapter 5 at Dowty's IT Division.

Frameworks for analysing and measuring competitive advantage can thus be used to gain a firmer grip over the otherwise messy stream of opportunities dealt with by an organization. This does not mean that the 'strategy' needs to be fixed and rigid – it may be partially well formed, partly fixed and partly completely open. Where the external (and for that matter, internal) environment is uncertain and turbulent it would be folly to have an overdesigned strategy, one with a high level of rigid commitment.[8] If that were the case, much of the financial value of the strategy would be quickly lost as soon as external events move against the company's (fixed) strategic posture.

Case study 3.2 Realizing that the fluid strategy is sometimes OK (Comet Technology)

During a review of internal capability of Comet Technology, the general manager was asked by leaders of a number of task forces to provide input on the top team's vision of the business strategy. He summoned the strategic facilitator and explained his concerns.

'The problem really comes down to this: We can see fairly clearly where we are going with our existing, core products. The problem is in emerging markets. When will they arrive? Who really knows? If we ask the customers, they say, "What can the technology do and what will it cost?" If we ask our operations people, they say "What level of sophistication will the customers want? What will our volumes be? How can we define the costs unless someone can give us an idea of volumes?" '

In the above case it was very difficult (although not hopelessly so) to make much progress in defining a well-articulated strategy for newer areas of opportunity. Scenario approaches (which will be explored in Chapter 7) might have been fruitful in this particular context, but the main point was that the general manager was nervous at unveiling a partially well-formed and partially unformed strategy to his managers. (Imagine a major car company unveiling its new model – without an engine – and saying 'we are still working on it'.) The embarrassment of partly formed strategy provides part of the reason why strategy is often so poorly communicated in organizations.

Competitive advantage in a changing environment

Competitive advantage is not static but is prone to change, often imperceptibly. One of the best stories told at business schools (for example, by Charles Handy) is that of the boiled frog. Apparently, if you put a frog in a pan of cold water and heat it up gradually it just swims around. Even when the water reaches boiling point the frog does not jump out and eventually it is dead. On the other hand, if you were to throw the frog into boiling water, it would jump out.

Exercise 3.2 Spotting the strategic frog (5 minutes)

Within your own or a past organization:

1. Can you identify any cases where a group of managers appear to have been trapped in a situation of incremental change to which they have not responded?
2. Over what period of time did the water first get hot, then reach boiling point?
3. What could they have done differently, when and how, to have avoided their final fate?

So, too, is 'competitive advantage' often eroded over time. Typically, it may take a long time for the full effects to be felt organizationally. Figure 3.1 illustrates the cycle of decline: notice how long it can take for a company to have its image impaired. Perceptions (externally and internally) of competitive strength can be highly misleading. This highlights the need to

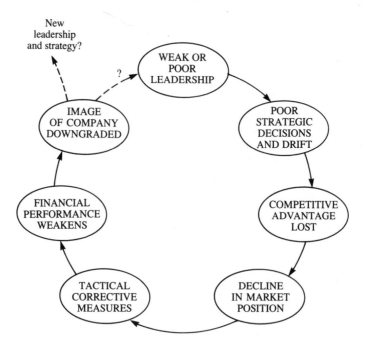

Figure 3.1 A cycle of strategic drift

measure competitive position – random judgements may have serious consequences leading to the following health warning:

> *Warning by the Institute for Safe Strategic Planning: Primitive, gut feel notions of unmeasured 'competitive advantage' can seriously damage your strategic health.*

It may take a long time for competitive advantage to be built up, and may take even longer to work through to improved financial performance and improved image. This can pose a particular problem in turnaround contexts, where financial turnaround (other than that based on shorter term cost-cutting) can lag on improvement in underlying competitive position.

In conclusion, competitive advantage is dynamic, rather than static, because of the:

- change and fluidity in expectations and requirements of customers
- change in the structure of the industry including distribution channels
- change in the strength of existing competitors
- effect of new entrants or substitutes
- change in the focus of the company, where the focus of the business may move to new, tougher markets
- economic and social change – for example, change in consumers' and industrial companies' attitudes towards premium-priced products and services in a growth period vs recession
- results of an internal change – for instance, a decline in capability as motivation becomes hard to sustain at levels of full stretch, owing to attrition of highly skilled staff, or simply to poor internal management and misguided cost-cutting.

These issues, in combination, highlight the need for ongoing strategic learning to pervade the organization. A one-off strategic plan or 'strategic review' often serves only to drain organizational energy and increase the aversion to strategic thinking. At best it may serve to catch up with what is not really known about the external environment and competitive position. I believe that the best approach is for strategic learning to be a continuous process of exploring key ways of sustaining competitive advantage.

Exercise 3.3   Analysing competitive advantage (20 minutes)

For your own organization:

1. Identify the key sources of competitive advantage that enabled it to establish itself originally as a significant player.
2. How has its competitive position been strengthened by continuing development of

its key capabilities? How has it been eroded (a) by internal sources of competitive disadvantage, or (b) by new, stronger players developing on entering the market?
3. What do you see as being the company's longer term future (a) if it continues on its present track, (b) if it were to deal decisively in renewing its key sources of competitive advantage?

The above exercise, if done thoroughly and honestly, may produce some important, challenging (and possibly disturbing) insights. But these insights may be at the heart of the organization's future – determining its success against drift or failure.

3.3 Learning about competitive advantage

Learning is a major source of competitive advantage precisely because it can be used to explore and develop that advantage. This learning process may go through a number of phases, including:

– conventional planning
– competitive analysis
– competitive bench-marking
– capability development.

The degree of reward and difficulty from each of these phases is illustrated in Figures 3.2 and 3.3.

Figure 3.2, which deals with incremental rewards, shows a number of key features:

1. Much of the incremental reward of conventional planning is achieved quickly and without creating a bureaucracy.
2. Competitive analysis typically results in disproportionate reward relative to effort. Some of this reward comes at an early stage in challenging existing views of the business (see the initial blip), but the main potential comes from deepening the analysis – shown in Figure 3.2 as a steep incline of reward.
3. Competitive bench-marking adds additional value but is shown here as having an incremental contribution comparable to conventional planning. This assumes, however, that competitive analysis is already in place – companies that have done no competitive analysis prior to bench-marking would show a much sharper return for their efforts.
4. Capability development shows a steady reward from its application.

Now compare this with Figure 3.3, which deals with the incremental difficulty of each evolutionary stage:

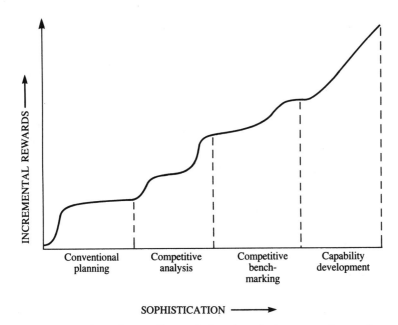

Figure 3.2 The four phases of strategic learning: the incremental rewards

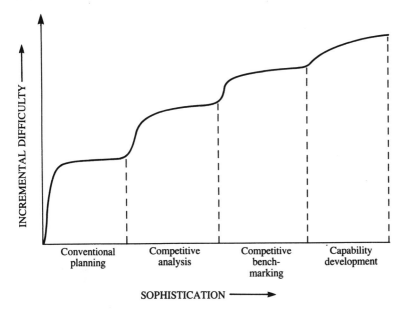

Figure 3.3 The four phases of strategic learning: the incremental difficulty

1. Conventional planning demands quite a lot of effort to introduce from scratch and this effort is large relative to the incremental reward (see Figure 3.2).
2. Competitor analysis requires a great deal of effort to set up initially, but this rapidly tapers off as it becomes more routine for managers.
3. Competitive bench-marking is seen as very difficult initially – often because managers are embarrassed to talk to other companies and share their views in depth. But again, this becomes easier as managers learn and gain in confidence.
4. Finally, capability development shows a smooth progression, as a continuous process.

Figures 3.2 and 3.3 therefore highlight the *choices* that are faced when an organization seeks to institutionalize strategic learning through specific processes. Although a good deal of benefit may accrue from simple and limited processes in more complex and changing environments, you will need to move a long way up the evolutionary ladder.

Conventional planning

Phase 1 (Figure 3.4) highlights learning via conventional planning routines. These may include, for example:

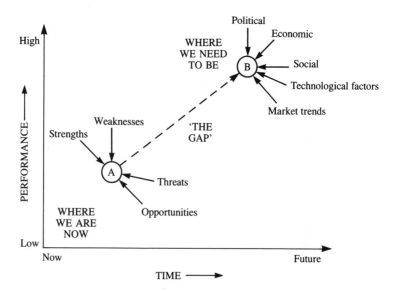

Figure 3.4 Conventional planning: the process

- setting barriers and financial objectives, and measuring 'the gap' between 'where we are now' and 'where we need to be' (or gap analysis)
- understanding 'where we are now' through strengths and weaknesses, opportunity and threats (SWOT) analysis
- exploring 'where we need to be' by looking at (a) the emerging threats, (b) changes in the wider political, economic, social and technological (PEST) environment and (c) market trends.

Where an organization has not spent much time formally reflecting on its strategic position and direction, conventional planning can, on its first introduction, produce significant learning benefits.

Case study 3.3   A management buy-out

During the buoyant late 1980s, the management team of a heavy engineering company, Meteor Engineering Limited, decided to launch a management buy-out as the holding company was seeking to divest the business. Working with a team of financial and business planning consultants, the managing director and financial director began work on a business plan for the buy-out.

While the resulting business plan was primarily operational and financial, with some overview of market prospects, some important issues and choices were revealed, for instance:

1. Meteor's business fell into two main areas: a commodity business doing routine repairs, and a more sporadic business of high-value, low-volume speciality manufactures. The margins of the routine repair business were weak, but those of the speciality business were very high. The problem was the unpredictability of the speciality work.
2. The business had relatively high fixed costs within its cost structure. This compounded the earlier problem of the volatility of speciality work.
3. The company lacked strong marketing and sales skills which would help expand turnover.
4. The company's cost base was high because of the costs of maintaining a large site, and also because of low labour productivity.

Although the financially based business plan did not reveal the full extent of the strategic (poor) health of the business, it did highlight some of the key issues that needed to be addressed. However, it fell short in suggesting that the strategic problems and constraints could be addressed by operational and financial measures alone.

The plan as it stood suggested expanding and gaining a better, more stable mix of business and also reducing costs and increasing productivity. But the result was that for the two years following the buy-out the business ran on a knife-edge and eventually had to be placed in receivership after two successive poor quarters.

Could things have been any different? With hindsight, the management team had set itself a near-impossible task of managing two quite different businesses with differing requirements via the same operational means. Had the team reflected longer upon their predicament they might have explored other options, such as:

- separating the two businesses (as Meteor Repair and Meteor Design) and developing more stand-alone strategies
- deciding to go for the commodity repairing business alone, and then seek a cost leadership position to gain economies of scale and boost productivity
- deciding to shut down and sell some of the site and then focus on the speciality manufacturing
- considering which other speciality activities they might service within the core and distinctive competencies of the business.

The lesson that this case reveals is that managers may spend some time reflecting upon their business position but may resume management action before they have really resolved the issues. The management alarm bells then ring, and the strategic learning promptly cuts out. This is a major problem when striving to gain strategic learning through more routine business and financial planning.

In the Meteor Engineering case we saw how conventional planning can yield insights when a company is at a strategic crossroads, but the overall picture emerging is often incomplete. In many cases, conventional planning falls short of even this degree of challenge, as it quickly becomes highly routinized. It often appears to be merely a ritual driven more by political forces than by business logic.

Moving into competitive analysis

A second, more advanced phase in developing strategic learning is that of *competitive analysis*, where a company tries to get a fix on its broad, competitive position. For instance, it may involve managers in the following:

1. Identify (formally) its key businesses – by product, market, technology and service functions. This may involve understanding much more about how 'the market' breaks into a number of different segments. Each of these segments can then be analysed in different, revealing ways.
2. For each (or a selection) of its 'key businesses', make some formal rating on whether the organization is 'on a par with', 'stronger than' or 'weaker than' its key competitors. This may need to be done by examining a specific number of key competitors.

Competitive analysis can reveal some powerful learning lessons which challenge existing views of the organization, and also of its key competitors.

Case study 3.4 Competitive analysis within a services environment – when strategic learning cuts out

A major services and distribution organization, the Galaxy Group, was concerned that it was not exploiting information systems for competitive advantage. It initiated a review of its current competitive position by drawing on a number of sources:

- interviews with sources of expert comment on the industry
- key suppliers of information systems to the industry
- interviews with managers internally, to gather their perceptions of company positioning.

This exercise was a major learning experience, not only for Galaxy managers, but also for the firm of strategy and information consultants commissioned to advise on this problem. For instance:

1. The purpose of interviewing managers internally *first* and external sources *second* was explained to Galaxy managers (in order to gain a measure of company beliefs *before* the external analysis – to highlight what had been learned). However, many managers grew impatient as to why this data collection was really necessary. They saw the project as being externally focused and little to do with their own perceptions and beliefs.
2. The joint client/consulting team became so absorbed in exploring the issues and collecting data that little time was spent in *conjecturing* 'what might we find out?' and 'what might the implications be?'. One of the consultants who kept nagging about this (sensitive) area was advised by his seniors to 'get on with the job and be sure we meet the client's deadline), echoing Argyris's findings elaborated earlier in this book.
3. As the project progressed it became transparent that the organization was indeed behind certain competitors in many of its approaches to exploiting information systems. Indeed, one of the leading companies in exploiting information systems was regarded by the client as lagging, but this was simply because its financial performance was poor. So powerful was the mindset in the client that the messages that might have come through loud and clear in the final presentation were toned down and muffled. On the safe side, the consultants who had done the work were excluded by their own consulting company from the presentation to the client as they were 'not senior enough'. This highlights how resistance to strategic learning both within a client and a firm of consultants can conspire with one another to dissipate challenge.
4. The issue of 'who your competitors are' is rarely non-trivial. The internal interviews revealed that very senior managers had a most limited view of competitive threat. They talked about the big, traditional players but not about new, more nimble entrants. Further, they did not seem to have digested major changes in the industry boundaries which meant they faced not just one but two, and possibly three, major types of competitor.
5. Many issues about organizational capability and resource base were raised. For

instance, the company's information systems staff led careers primarily if not exclusively within a central IT function. Rarely did their career paths rotate through services/line management.

Also, there was considerable resistance within Galaxy to acquiring software packages that might have (a) accelerated developments and (b) reduced costs considerably. The reluctance to investigate these options appeared to derive from underlying fears. These concerned the implications of procuring more software packages externally in terms of restructuring and subsequent job losses. (Again, we find here the action loop blocking the learning loop from Chapter 2.)

Again, this case highlights that although competitive analysis was *potentially* a powerful vehicle for strategic learning, the learning tended to close down in the face of perceived threat. This generates an important, if fairly obvious, insight – that learning is not merely a cognitive process that takes inputs, processes them and yields outputs; it is a process where managers anticipate (albeit imperfectly) the implications of what they are learning ahead of themselves. It is thus a process that *works forwards* to anticipate practical implications. Sometimes the anticipated results of the learning process may even ripple backwards to inhibit the learning process itself.

Strategic learning is thus inseparable ultimately from the process of change. The learning process is certainly not a purely intellectual activity. It is very much a process infused with feelings and possibly fears that need to be managed.

In many ways our rationalist Western culture does management a profound disservice by playing down the role of feeling, intuition and instinct. This Western rationalist culture sees managers (still) largely as rational actors. Yet managers are not merely rational decision makers, they are humans who in turn are driven by instincts such as territorial protection. Much of what actually happens in management needs to be understood in terms of instincts and feelings – and also in terms of culture. This means that strategic learning, too, cannot be purely a 'rational' process but must embrace the intuitive side of management. We must also recognize the instinctive forces at work that shape organizational change.

Advancing into competitive bench-marking

The third phase of strategic learning for competitive advantage is that of competitive bench-marking. Unlike competitive analysis, which is often broadly based and undertaken as a one-off exercise, competitive bench-marking builds strategic learning into management's planning, monitoring and control routines. Instead of being an adjunct to 'how we do things around here' (the organizational paradigm), it becomes integral with it.

Many attempts at competitive bench-marking falter, however, because they are seen as something 'nice to do'. Take, for example, the following case, where there were some clear breakthroughs in perception of the company but only a subset appeared to be translated into change.

Case study 3.5   Bench-marking and networking by a financial services company

Over a six-month period, half of the senior managers of a financial services company, the Nova Group, sought to bench-mark companies in the same and also in different industries. They wanted to tackle a very difficult issue: How do companies with complex business processes seek to (a) increase customer responsiveness, (b) simplify processes, (c) improve staff responsiveness, (d) reduce staff numbers, and achieve these things simultaneously and smoothly?

Nova's managers visited and received exchange visits from four other major organizations. A number of key insights came from this project, as follows:

1. *Incremental insights*: these were easily integrated into managers' ways of thinking about change – for instance, that the process of reviewing staff capability was not just a one-off requirement, but was needed continuously.
2. *Strategic insights*: that the process redesign currently achieved was not sufficiently radical or far-reaching to achieve the organization's stretching objectives.

In the months following the review it was unclear whether these insights had been fully captured and assimilated as no specific decisions reflecting these insights seem to have crystallized. However, it is possible that these learning insights had gone into suspense. They might subsequently have been re-awakened, for example, by renewed pressure for organizational change.

This case highlights the problem of linking learning to decision-making and change. It is conceivable that this strategic learning might become re-engaged in the change process at a future stage. However, it is possible that by the time an opportunity for action had crystallized, it would have decayed and disintegrated. Thus, where the unlearning curve is steep, earlier and much greater amplification appears necessary to achieve resulting benefit. Although the full potential of competitive bench-marking was not realized in this case, it highlights that bench-marking can provide a valuable fix on the organization's underlying source of competitive advantage.

Before leaving this third phase, a useful framework for capturing and analysing issues that surface as a result of bench-marking is shown in Figure 3.5. This framework should be used to plan and to learn from bench-marking exercises.

Figure 3.5 analyses the business impact on the vertical axis (again, as

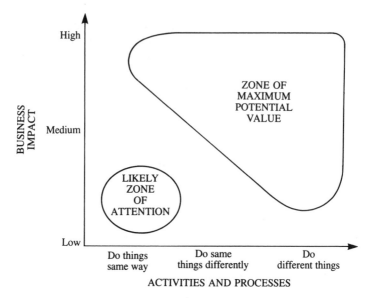

Figure 3.5 Analysing the results from bench-marking

'high', 'medium' or 'low') and, on the horizontal axis, differentiates between:

- doing things the same way
- doing the same things, but differently
- doing different things.

The third category, 'doing different things', may include not merely things that another company is doing and your organization is *not* doing, but also those that you *are* doing and the other company *is* not doing. The latter case may yield significant clues to underlying sources of competitive advantage or disadvantage. For instance, you might be performing a lot of activities that another company is not doing at all, and these may enable the other company to streamline how it adds value at least cost and in the least time to its customers.

The zone of greatest interest in Figure 3.5 (the top right-hand corner) may thus extend right down to areas that are perceived as being of low business impact. This zone is drawn deliberately to the right-hand side of the matrix as managers will often focus on the area to the bottom left-hand corner quadrant. Often their attention is devoted to *confirming* what they are doing against 'best practice' elsewhere, rather than to exploring and understanding differences. They may also be inclined to analyse issues of lesser business impact rather than the more important areas.

Capability development

In the fourth phase of capability development, competitive analysis and bench-marking are geared directly to improving the internal capability of the organization. In this phase, competitive analysis and bench-marking are both central, driving ingredients in planning and control processes. Also, these processes in turn are geared towards developing capability as opposed to purely producing a set of financial or non-financial targets or measures. We take a much closer look at how capability can be developed in both the Dowty and Mercury Communications cases in Part Two.

Exercise 3.4   Phases of strategic learning (5 minutes)

Would you describe the current phase of strategic learning for competitive advantage in your organization as being mainly in the:

(a) routine planning and control phase?
(b) competitive analysis phase?
(c) competitive bench-marking phase?
(d) capability development phase (suitably steered by inputs from phases (b) and (c)?

Where you are mainly in phase (a), are there implications of focusing primarily on routine planning and controls in terms of narrowing external vision, identifying competitive decline and avoiding internal drift?

3.4   Creating multiple layers of competitive advantage

Competing by differentiation versus cost

If we look at earlier and more formal ideas of competitive advantage (for instance, Porter[2]) they appear to suggest that companies must choose between opposite strategies in order to be successful. For instance, Porter suggests that differing generic strategies (or 'competitive styles'[6]) may be available across industries. Notably a company may compete primarily with a differentiated value that it offers its customers, or on the basis of driving its costs down to have the lowest cost levels in the industry. Porter suggests that, with very few exceptions, these kinds of strategy are mutually exclusive. He argues that if you try to do a mixture of both – and particularly if you try to cover a broad range of products while also emphasizing a few key products (a 'focus' strategy) – then you fall between all the various strategic schools. Porter calls this graphically 'stuck in the middle'.

What he *does not* say, however, is that if you differentiate then costs do not matter – because they still do. Nor does he say that if you pursue cost leadership then you do not deliver a level of value or quality comparable to industry standards.

Porter's typology appears to work best where the strategic terrain is uneven and where differences in value added and cost levels between key players are both significant and readily measurable. For instance, the car industry in the 1980s had clear examples of differentiated players (BMW, Jaguar) versus cost leadership companies (certain Japanese companies and East European). But by the 1990s these distinctions have become more difficult to make. For instance, Toyota has launched such models as the Lexus against such traditional manufacturers as BMW, threatening BMW's differentiated position. Japanese cars now sometimes command an exclusive price premium, rather than one being seen as cheaper substitutes. The neater distinctions cut by Porter have become more blurred and ambiguous, especially when one is dealing with a fiercely competitive, mature industry. Once again, this puts a premium value on strategic learning.

The car industry is not an unusual exception. In many industries the notion that these are relatively simple routes to competitive edge simply do not apply in management practice. Although Porter never said that generic strategies were the necessary *and sufficient* ingredients for competitive strategy, increasingly managers need to seek not so much single sources of core advantage but multiple *and reinforcing* sources. The successful company needs to build a *system* of competitive advantage, and one that is continually renewing itself.

To some extent, therefore, management thinking has moved on from Porter. Practitioners and theorists realize that the ideal strategies of Porter are often of no real assistance in evolving *business-specific* sources of competitive advantage.

Seeking sustainable advantage

Although Porter's disciples (e.g. Ghemawat[7]) emphasized *sustainability* of competitive advantage, this can again suggest that the key task is to protect competitive advantage once this has been gained. The danger is that competitive advantage is regarded as a 'thing' that you create and then maintain or develop. Many sources of competitive advantage are, however, less tangible. They are continually being recreated, frequently on a daily basis. In particular, sources of advantage such as

– building corporate image
– responsiveness to customer demands externally

- internal responsiveness
- problem diagnosis and solving – whether this is tactical or strategic
- capturing and evaluating and exploiting new business opportunity

are ongoing processes, and need to be tracked via strategic learning.

These processes are becoming increasingly important relative to more tangible sources of advantage: e.g. assets, market share, products. This shift occurs as the service element in value added by the business goes up, and as businesses become more complex and interdependent.

Strategic learning provides a key strand that holds the above, softer sources of competitive advantage together. In all of these less tangible sources of competitive advantage, learning about the wider issues involved in problems and opportunities helps improve the responsiveness of the business system. In the long run, softer sources of competitive advantage may account for the majority of variance in the performance of companies in the same sector. This is not to say that the more difficult sources of competitive advantage are unimportant, they clearly are; but the software of competitive advantage is becoming primary in many cases. Tangible sources of competitive advantage allow you access to the pitch in a meaningful way, but the 'competitive game' is decided by the softer sources of advantage – especially in the long run.

A further useful input is that of time-based competitive advantage.[8] Although this school of thought probably makes too many claims for the benefits gained by speeding up processes, responsiveness and flexibility are clearly important factors for the successful organization. The following list gives some important illustrations of how time (or speed) plays a major influence in shaping competitive advantage:

- reducing the length of time taken to develop and launch a new product or service
- faster yet smoother integration of new acquisitions
- quicker turnaround time of customer enquiries and confirmation of transactions
- accelerating major change programmes through the use of task forces and by project management
- speeding up the business planning cycle without undermining the quality of decision-making.

Speeding activities up without detriment to quality and without increasing costs demands much more effective learning and feedback in the management process. Without continual and shared learning, acceleration of processes may lead to costly errors.

Time-based competitive advantage has close resemblances to some key themes within project management reborn. Traditionally managers coordinate activities by thinking about quality, cost and time as separate issues. Project management tells us that these three issues or variables trade-off against each other. To illustrate this, where there is continual attention to quality cost may be neglected and overlooked. Equally, where attention to cost is obsessive, quality often deteriorates. Even rarer do managers keep as strong a grip on *time* as a competitive weapon. More conventionally, where a process is accelerated it is thought that costs will increase due to problems associated with activity compression. However, costs can often be *reduced* by accelerating activity. In addition, customer value can be *increased* by accelerating activities. At any point in time the organization knows more about its environment than its key rivals as it has more time to spend on strategic issues. It is thus in a better position to satisfy customer needs.

Also, the organization may be able to deliver a more responsive service which can, in turn, reduce customers' costs or risks. This might be converted either into premium pricing or into greater volumes, alternatively the tendency for customers to switch to other suppliers can be reduced, or a mixture of all three of these factors.

Exercise 3.5   Competitive advantage (15 minutes)

What do you see as being the unique or distinctive sources of competitive advantage of your company? For instance, you may wish to consider:

- market image
- products
- services
- technologies
- distribution channels
- market share or focus
- customer responsiveness
- financial strengths
- management resources
- systems infrastructure
- low cost base, etc.

What makes you think these are unique or distinctive? How do these reinforce one another?

If you are struggling to find sources of unique or distinctive advantage, does this tell you something about your longer-term vulnerability, or indeed why you are struggling currently to achieve adequate levels of performance?

You may discover from this exercise that you could be losing your traditional base of competitive advantage. Alternatively, your organization may have achieved a strong competitive position but is now at a peak of achievement that is difficult to sustain. This can present its own problems. Often the organization can grow stale, and possibly complacent, through having achieved its earlier objectives.

On the other hand, your company may require turnaround and may have to revitalize itself from the core outwards. Regardless of whether or not you are personally at the centre of leading this change, it may be very worth while making these reflections. Your own future career strategy will inevitably be impacted on by any underlying decay in competitive position.

This now brings us to the topic of how strategic learning can be used to manage internal dynamics within the organization – managing change through strategic learning.

3.5 Managing internal dynamics through strategic learning

So far we have focused on exploring mainly the *external* aspects of competitive advantage and strategic learning, but strategic learning can be just as powerful in steering internal change. This section looks at three key questions:

1. Is change seen as a learning process, and if not should it be?
2. If so, how can we manage change more effectively through strategic learning?
3. What are the benefits of fusing strategic learning and the change process together?

Change as a learning process

Change appears to be often seen as primarily bound up with management action rather than integral with learning of individual managers, teams and the wider organization. This is perhaps a reflection of the management style that pervades many companies. This style is neatly captured in the approach to targeting change activities of

SHOOT, then
AIM, then
LOAD

which appears to be prevalent in many, if not most, organizations.

A model of how change might be managed as a learning process is shown in Figure 3.6. This highlights:

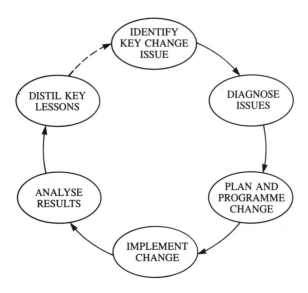

Figure 3.6   A change and learning loop (1)

2. A change issue may crystallize; for instance, a reorganization is seen as being necessary, or communication is seen as being poor and requiring improvement.
3. The sub-issues involved within this problem or opportunity are analysed. These may include, for example, the likely costs/benefits/risks of change, the barriers and enabling factors that may accelerate or retard the change, the likelihood that this change may be overtaken by events, and so on.
4. A viable change strategy may then emerge which needs to be made into a coherent plan and be fully programmed.
5. The change has then to be mobilized into implementation.
6. The results of change need to be analysed. Were the benefits achieved, and at what cost and risk? If they were not, why not?
7. The key lessons can be distilled for the future. These may embrace how change is managed generally in the organization and also how more specific areas of capability can be developed.

Exercise 3.6   Change as a learning process (10 minutes)

To what extent do managers manage change as a strategic learning process, along the lines of Figure 3.6, in your own organization? In which phases is this process in the organization generally strongest or weakest? What does this imply about the organizational style, and also the style of key individuals steering change?

I suspect that in many cases this reveals that learning is often impeded and is seen as a peripheral ingredient during the change process. Even the learning that does occur may be blocked or undermined at key phases of the change. For example, during the diagnosis of change issues may be too narrow; or the planning and programming of change may be effective, but so much effort is spent on implementation that results of the change are not well analysed and measured. Also, rarely will the key lessons be distilled and disseminated freely and openly to key stakeholders. Is this a correct portrayal of the results of your own exercise?

Figure 3.6 thus gives you a useful process for understanding how change can be managed via strategic learning. But although it shows how change is iterative or 'loop-like', it does not by itself highlight the specific *iterations* that may go on through this process. Figure 3.7 shows what typically occurs as managers reflect on what they have learned through the change process. This highlights that:

1. During the diagnosis, it is common to redefine the main issue at the core of the change. For instance, what was the underlying rationale of the change? What benefits were targeted? How does this change link to other areas of change and how important is it relative to other change thrusts?
2. During the planning and programming phase, further clarity may be gained by analysing those issues that are most important or most difficult to address.

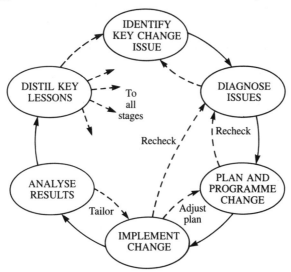

Figure 3.7 A change and learning loop (2)

3. During implementation, the change plan or programme is likely to need to be adjusted and reshaped as new data are uncovered. Although, ideally, all key data should be analysed in advance for successful project management and to minimize in-flight changes, the *learning* and thus fluid nature of change management makes this goal an ideal.

This feature also suggests that a more flexible style of project management needs to be applied in helping managing change than that described in many conventional texts, especially by:

- analysing the results of change continually throughout the different phases of change – which involves continual feedback (and thus learning) throughout implementation;
- distilling key learning lessons – which involves reflecting on *all stages* of the change: diagnosis, planning, implementation and analysis of the end results.

Culture change and strategic learning

The process of welding together strategic learning, managing change and more fluid, project management is best illustrated by the following case study.

Case study 3.6   Culture change in a large, integrated group – Red Giant International

A major multinational Group, which we shall call Red Giant International, began a culture change programme that was aimed at making managers more flexible, friendly and responsive. The objective of this change was to cut out: (a) the inefficiency and ineffectiveness that resulted from duplication of activities, (b) unnecessary complexity and bureaucracy, and (c) the need for 'second guessing' by managers at all levels, if Red Giant was to survive. This change went through the following learning sequence.

1. Senior management (led by the top manager) identified this as an area of concern.
2. Initial diagnosis was undertaken through an employee attitude survey. This revealed low morale as the result of continual internal battling against 'the system'.
3. The change issue was redefined to be a problem involving not merely having an inappropriate structure (and supporting systems) but also one of culture. The issue was thus redefined as being one of *culture change*.
4. The top strata of managers within Red Giant was then gathered together to review this diagnosis of issues. Some provocative plans and programmes for change were then put forward by the top manager in order to gain momentum for change.

5. Following these initial meetings, a more detailed change plan was established which set up a series of culture change task forces. These had an ongoing remit to facilitate change.
6. Implementation was then launched, initially through a series of diagnosis workshops. In parallel, personal counselling of key individuals was initiated. During this period the change process had to be adjusted on a number of occasions – for instance, to give the workshops a more behavioural rather than a cerebral bite.
7. Results were collected and analysed by conducting further attitude surveys periodically to gain 'hard' measures of progress. Also, key breakthroughs were identified which appeared to be directly or indirectly attributable to the culture change programme (or 'softer' measures). At this point, a number of key stories of breakthroughs were collected and evaluated, and fed back to confirm that tangible benefits had been achieved.
8. Some of the key lessons were then distilled from this programme. One of the lessons was that the time-scales to make deliberate culture change take root can be very long. The danger is that the duration of change is longer than the attention and commitment span of the organization and of the longevity of key stakeholders, including the leadership. Another lesson was that expectations that culture change would not be 'all fun' were not set sufficiently clearly at the outset.

Following on from the Red Giant case we can now examine the wider issues and systems with which this learning and change process interfaced. These are shown in Figure 3.8, highlighting a number of relationships.

1. The corporate and business strategy ought to highlight the need for change. Indeed, planning, learning and change should be seen as an integral process of 'PLC' ('P' for planning, 'L' for learning, and 'C' for change). Learning is the glue that links successful planning with successful change management. In the Red Giant case above, for example, the culture change programme was preceded by a strategy review. This review had already put in progress a programme of simplifying the existing businesses. There was therefore less need for a complex bureaucracy than was previously the case.
2. The change issue being focused on should be defined in such a way as to integrate with other programmes of operational and organizational change and development. For instance, the culture change initiative in the earlier case overlapped with quality management and attempts to build a market-led culture.
3. Diagnosis issues may incorporate and connect a range of items, including people issues, and the impact on organizational structure, style and systems. In the Red Giant case, the implementation of advanced office

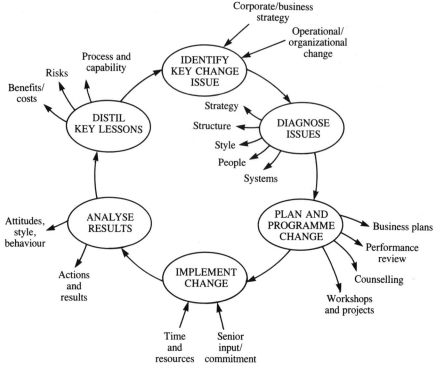

Figure 3.8 The learning and change context

automation facilitated a reduction in staff numbers, a reduction of meetings and committees and paved the way for more effective cross-functional networking.

4. Planning and programming may exploit a range of vehicles including business plans, performance reviews, and, as in the Red Giant case, by workshops and counselling. This may also incorporate a team-building element.

5. Implementing change requires the input of senior management and their ongoing commitment and appropriate resources and time. In cases where senior managers do not devote enough sustained attention to change, then a loss of momentum and direction is very likely. This often results in change having to be restarted at a later stage.

6. Analysis of results needs to cover the *hard* outputs (changes in measured business and financial performance) and *soft* outputs (attitudes, behaviours and styles).

7. Distilling key lessons may cover not just the final results (benefits and costs) but also the risks undergone. It should also cover lessons on how the change and learning *process* has been managed. It may also highlight more visibly than previously the strengths and weaknesses in the organization's capability.

From the Red Giant case it is clear that deliberate culture change is a classic example of strategic learning. It is also a particularly difficult application as it involves sustaining the learning over a considerable period (depth) and throughout the organization (breadth).

Exercise 3.7 Evaluating a past area of change (10 minutes)

For a particular major area of change initiated in your business in the last twelve months, to what extent have the interfaces with other systems in the organization (such as business planning, human resources management, top management involvement, control and learning processes) been integrated as in the Red Giant example? If the level of integration was perhaps weak, what were the consequences of this (a) in terms of the benefits delivered (and at what cost and risk) and (b) in terms of the difficulty experienced in the change process?

From this section on change as a learning process, we have therefore seen how strategic learning can be used to steer and facilitate change. Where change *is seen* explicitly as a learning process, this can substantially reduce the problems of error denial or 'self-sealing errors' which Argyris highlighted for us previously.

From the earlier Red Giant case on cultural change, it is transparent that not only do we have to manage action in organizations, we also need to manage the learning process. But this also means that we have to manage feelings. We need to be able to share our feelings about 'errors' without setting up a vicious cycle of blame. We must be able to do this without over-anaesthetizing ourselves to errors, rationalizing the mistakes by exaggerating achievements and putting failure down to the 'uncontrollables'.

In many organizations managers are not very good at handling the feelings associated with making strategic learning effective – especially those involved in admitting to errors. But unless these underlying feelings can be managed learning is likely to remain isolated. Strategic learning will otherwise continue in island form, rather than in the form of continents in the organization.

3.6 Synthesis and conclusions

This ends our discussion on how learning can lead to dynamic, and self-reinforcing competitive advantage. We began this discussion by arguing that competitive advantage is a critical ingredient in creating a successful business strategy. In order to identify and create competitive advantage, strategic learning was found to be an essential force in isolating key competitive strengths and weaknesses.

We also saw the importance of using strategic learning to reshape business strategy, rather than allow business strategy to become entombed in rigid planning routines that then drive out the learning.

Some welcome news was that the notion of 'competitive advantage' is relatively easy to grasp – indeed, it resolves some of the problems associated with the label of 'strategy', and helps to break down the slightly artificial barriers between strategic and operational management, thus dissolving this false dichotomy (where rigidly made).

The notion of competitive advantage was then examined more closely, and this concept was found to be more fluid than that suggested by some of the classic strategy texts. In learning about competitive advantage different phases include formal planning, competitive analysis, competitive bench-marking and capability development. All these stages were potentially fruitful. The later stages, such as competitive bench-marking and capability development, might initially appear to be more difficult but are likely to yield greater and more sustainable rewards.

This also led to the notion of multiple and reinforcing layers of competitive advantage. This was seen to be more powerful and relevant than Porter's 'generic strategies' (although that is not to say that these generic strategies are not useful as a general framework). When looked at in a dynamic context, learning was useful in revealing changes in more fluid competitive advantage. Learning also helped expedite and focus key management decision processes, being an important source of advantage in its own right.

We then saw how the internal dynamics of change in the organization could be looked upon as an opportunity for strategic learning. If implementation of major change is to be achieved effectively, then implementation must be managed explicitly as a learning process. As many organizations are currently undergoing major transformation in order to remain or restore competitive advantage, blending strategic learning with the change process becomes a critical factor in achieving competitive success.

We shall conclude with a simple framework for strategic analysis which codifies the broad thinking of this chapter at a macro level. This tool is that of STAIR:

S for **simple**, clear and coherent **strategy**
T for **timing** (which needs to be appropriate)
A for **advantage** (which needs to be multiple, reinforcing and sustainable)
I for quality of **implementation**, which must be effective
R for adequate **resources** and underlying capability.

Figure 3.9 gives a pictorial view of the STAIR tool. The underlying idea is that for strategic success you need to have each of these individual elements lined up. I shall leave you to think about some of your successful versus less successful past strategies, to see how they compare using the STAIR tool. The STAIR tool can also be used to screen strategic options currently being faced. The advantage of STAIR is that it is simple and memorable yet more powerful than SWOT analysis; it is also more implementation-oriented than most other analysis tools.

In Part Two we shall look in rather more depth at the choice of learning vehicles. This then equips us to deal with specific applications in Part Three.

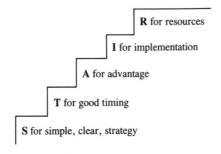

Figure 3.9 STAIR analysis: testing your strategy

References

1. Ohmae, K., *The Mind of the Strategist*, McGraw-Hill, New York, 1982.
2. Porter, E. M., *Competitive Strategy*, The Free Press, New York, 1980.
3. Porter, E. M., *Competitive Advantage*, The Free Press, New York, 1985.
4. Quinn, J. B., *Strategies for Change: Logical Incrementalism*, Richard D. Irwin, Illinois, 1980.
5. Mintzberg, H., 'Patterns in strategy formation, *Management Science*, May 1978, pp. 934–48.
6. Grundy, A. N., *Corporate Strategy and Financial Decisions*, Kogan Page, 1992.
7. Ghemawat, P., 'Sustainable advantage', *Harvard Business Review*, September–October 1986, pp. 53–8.
8. Stalk, G., *Competing Against Time*, Free Press, 1990.

PART TWO
FACILITATING THE LEARNING PROCESS

4
Choosing the delivery vehicle

4.1 Learning options

This chapter explores the choices for implementing strategic learning. We begin by diagnosing the problems or opportunities that you may be able to tackle and discuss the selection of different kinds of 'delivery vehicle'. We then define the key outputs, process and inputs. This is achieved by working *backwards* from targeted benefits to design the process. But first let us take a look at the problems and opportunities.

4.2 Diagnosing the problem or opportunity

A wide diversity of possible agendas for strategic learning exists at any one time. For instance, you may have at any one time a variety of possible targets, including:

- scanning of the wider business environment
- evaluating a specific new business opportunity
- conducting a review of business activities
- analysing how specific areas of change are or should be, managed
- investigating areas where performance can or must be improved.

Scanning the environment

Here a wide variety of options open up. At the broadest level you may wish to look at how the industry environment as a whole may be changing. The trigger for this might be, for instance, environmental pressures, major technology change, market saturation and maturity or regulating impact.

This exercise might be done either with a shorter-term (or medium-term) focus or with a longer-term focus. This option is represented in the top two quadrants in the matrix shown in Figure 4.1. You might prefer to focus on a scenario specific to a particular decision; for instance, you may wish to consider a scenario for a longer-term investment decision. Alternatively, you may seek an overview of the environment for a product launch where the time-scales are of shorter duration. Another example in the bottom left-hand quadrant would be that of regulatory change and its shorter-term impact on likely restructuring in a particular business unit.

Figure 4.1 therefore indicates that scanning can be done for a range of applications. These choices need to be prioritized so that managers do not overstretch themselves and seek to scan the world. Equally, building too narrow and specific a scenario may result in a myopic view of the environment.

In the aero-engine industry, for instance, scenarios could be devised by way of a wide range of scanning exercises; for example:

- broad/shorter-term (in the upper left-hand quadrant): an analysis of the possible impact of economic downturn (or upturn) on the structure of your industry;
- broad/longer-term (in the upper right-hand quadrant): a view of your industry post-2000, possibly with high international political volatility, an increased emphasis on energy conservation, and higher fuel costs;
- specific/longer-term (in the lower right-hand quadrant): a scenario of factors affecting demand for mid-range sized civil airliners (and engine characteristics) post-2000;
- specific/shorter-term (in the lower left-hand quadrant): demand potential for a specific product, including factors inhibiting versus boosting demand.

	SHORTER TERM	LONGER TERM
BROAD	Shorter term Industry-wide scenario	Longer term Industry-wide scenario
SPECIFIC	Product launch	Longer term investment decision

Figure 4.1 Scanning matrix (with examples)

Exercise 4.1   Exploring the business environment (5 minutes)

Brainstorm a number of possible applications of strategic learning for your business which involve scanning the environment:

1. Into which of the quadrants do these fall?
2. Which issues are likely to have most impact?
3. Which involve greatest uncertainty?
4. For one of these issues, what are the *specific benefits* that you can target out of a strategic learning exercise?
5. Who might you wish to involve in the exercise, how and when?

Evaluating a specific, new business opportunity

In any company there is likely to be a large number of opportunities that the business could exploit. This we can usefully call its *opportunity set*. In addition to the existing cash stream, the opportunity set is an integral part of the value of the business and these opportunities, if exploited successfully, will generate future (net) cash flow.

There is also a flow of *potential* opportunities, which is the *opportunity stream*. The opportunity stream is the flow of possibilities for future business development. This flow occurs naturally as a result of the business product/market position and its capacity to shape customer needs proactively. It is also dependent on the organization's capability to convert these opportunities into profitable business propositions.

Evaluating new business opportunity lends itself naturally to strategic learning, but the ability to generate and sift the opportunity stream depends very much on organizational structure and style.

Case study 4.1   Innovation and learning

A European food company invited a visitor from Japan to visit its facilities to compare approaches to product development and innovation. After a day in discussion with a diversity of managers, the Japanese visitor was asked to be quite open and to feed back his impressions.

What followed left the European managers stunned. The Japanese manager said: 'The best way to illustrate the differences between how we and you do things, which are enormous, is by just showing you this ...'

The Japanese manager then reached over and took a box of tissues from the office. He then proceeded to pluck them out of the box one by one and throw each into the air. Within 40 seconds he had emptied half the box leaving his European audience wondering what on earth he was doing. He continued: 'You see, you have so few ideas, and when you do have them you hang on to them and spend, oh, so very long on them. We do it differently. As you can see, we produce a continual stream of ideas, of opportunities. We don't pursue all of them, nor do we pick everything up immediately. But we always have a surplus of ideas for improvement.'

The European reader may recoil from this story because of the feeling that a free-flowing opportunity stream may simply overwhelm managers. But if you have an appropriate filter for sifting new ideas, then it ought to be feasible to deal with this stream.

There are many possible areas that may serve as strategic learning exercises for new business development. These may include, for instance:

- account penetration
- acquisitions
- alliances and joint ventures
- customer relationships – development
- distribution channels (new)
- licensing or franchise arrangements
- market entry or development
- product/technology development
- service development
- systems integration (with customers).

Although some of the above items may be relatively self-evident, others may be less so. For instance, ideas such as developing customer relationships, service development, or systems integration, may not immediately spring to mind. Yet these areas may yield greater and more sustainable possibilities for competitive advantage. Equally, if acquisitions spring to mind these may then drive out thinking about alliances, joint ventures and licensing or franchise arrangements.

Again, you may feel it unwise to amass too many possible ideas, but narrowing the focus may lead to a myopic view of possible areas for business development. Ultimately this kind of narrow thinking may lead to a bankrupt, corporate mind.

Obviously this raises the issue of how a surplus of opportunities can be prioritized.

Exercise 4.2   Prioritizing business development ideas (10 minutes)

List a few existing business development opportunities that might be used as strategic learning exercises. For *two* of these opportunities:

1. What is the precise nature of the opportunity? (Consider which of the headings of business development it impinges on.)

2. How important is it perceived to be by the company?
3. How important *should it be* perceived to be?
4. Who might be involved in evaluating the opportunity as a learning exercise?
5. Who might be asked to champion or critique this within senior management?

It is very worthwhile to conduct the above exercise for *two* opportunities. This should yield a good indication of the kinds of strategic learning exercise that have most chances of viability. By looking at two areas you will be able to identify some important contrasts.

Conducting a wider review of business activities

Moving beyond evaluation of a specific business opportunity, you may elect to consider a much broader review of the businesses you conduct. Inevitably this type of exercise involves a different kind of positioning in the organization to that of a discrete new business development alone. Whereas most evaluations of new business opportunity are likely to be non-life-threatening, wider reviews of business activities inevitably provoke concern.

If a *strategic* business review is conducted as an open learning exercise, then this should promote perceptions of fairness amongst managers and staff. A strategic review in which senior managers listen and learn from divers inputs – both vertically and horizontally within the organization – paves the way to much smoother and better targeted implementation.

The key benefits of applying strategic learning to a review of all businesses occur through:

– identifying business areas that do not have genuine fit to the capabilities of the Group or have problems of competitive decline
– inhibiting ill-advised strategic moves that might otherwise significantly blunt corporate performance
– focusing development efforts on a more limited number of areas so that adequate time and resources are spent in restoring competitive advantage.

Options for strategic learning vehicles to conduct a wide-ranging business review include:

1. *Top-level learning*: for instance, initiating a top team strategic workshop focusing on (a) broad competitive positioning of business units and market attractiveness, followed by (b) more detailed probing of 'strategic hot spots'. These may include those businesses which offer major upside opportunities or may involve businesses in which there are major downsides.

2. *Top-down and bottom-up learning*: for example, setting up an initial workshop by top managers to define key issues and questions. This can be followed by project work by middle and other managers on key issues. Outputs can then be shared in mini workshops prior to feeding upwards. These outputs are then tested by the top team.
3. *Three-way learning*: by blending the top-down, bottom-up and horizontal approaches above. This adds the extra ingredient of horizontal interchange which facilitates cross-functional team-working.

The third option (three-way learning) is the most complex but is also usually the most effective way of securing rounded learning. Where managers are skilled at analysing strategic issues, this process can be relatively quick – it may also considerably pave the way for more rapid implementation of any change.

Exercise 4.3   Project managing a strategic review (15 minutes)

Let us suppose that your chief executive decides to embark on a major, strategic review of the range of businesses. Because of your interest in strategic learning, he or she chooses *you* to project-manage the review process:

1. Which of the three options above would you advise him or her to choose, and why?
2. On which specific issues would you wish to spend *most* and *least* time?
3. How many project groups would you wish to set up to cover the key issues without producing 'strategic indigestion'? On what specific issues would these focus?

During the above exercise you may have encountered the following problems:

1. While you may ideally like to involve as many managers as possible, you may be concerned that will prove unacceptable or unsustainable. So how will you resolve the dilemma between (a) achieving a robust process while (b) also gaining sufficient commitment and support?
2. You may have struggled to define the 'key issues'. Either (a) you defined only a few issues that seemed to cover just a part of the real agenda, or (b) you defined far too many.

There is no simple answer to either of the above dilemmas. The best way to approach it is to produce a first proposal and then test it from a number of different angles to arrive at something that makes sense.

It is often useful to do a quick design and leave it for a day or so. In the meantime some remote part of your brain will be refining the approach, drawing in ideas and testing them, and possibly questioning your existing assumptions. This highlights the importance of marshalling your *subconscious learning* resources. Every good thinker (and manager) knows the virtue of tapping into subconscious or semi-conscious learning processes.

Analysing areas of key change

We now move on to another key issue: analysing change. In the 1990s few organizations (and managers) have been untouched by major external and internal change. I believe that few companies have succeeded in dealing with change effectively, and most appear still to be struggling with what may sometimes seem like an octopus of change. Even where changes are forced through this often occurs without:

– thinking through, and then managing the impact of internal change on external competitive position; for instance, inappropriate cost-cutting may undermine customer service
– focusing on the 'soft' as well as the 'hard' aspects of change (which includes structure, systems and perhaps the head-count); softer factors, including culture, style, and skills, are often neglected
– managing change as an integrated programme: typically change is managed piecemeal and without any real sense of overall direction being communicated.

Case study 4.2   Lunarware

A leading UK retailer, Lunarware, introduced advanced information systems to secure just-in-time stocks and a facility to achieve rapid reorders. This gave it the capacity to achieve significant competitive advantage through:

– lower stock levels
– higher sales of faster-moving items
– lower mark-downs of slower-moving stocks
– higher customer satisfaction through fast re-supply of popular lines
– lower central overheads.

The new systems were implemented along in-house project management lines. Yet some months later a number of problems arose in a busy seasonal period. Some very important lines were out of stock, losing not only sales but also threatening the company's image of itself as a 'reliable, quality retailer'.

A top manager then launched an initiative to find out why these stock-outs had happened. The findings of this initiative implied that the relevant departments were not commercial enough – it was felt that they were simply not being entrepreneurial.

A programme was then set in place to broaden the commercial and risk-taking skills of staff to enable them to develop a 'culture of being entrepreneurial'. Unfortunately, staff already considered themselves to be 'commercial', although they accepted that risk-taking was unevenly rewarded in the organization.

The programme was aborted after the first pilot workshop when it became rapidly clear to the company that this programme was – at least to them – a solution chasing a problem.

Although this retail case reads like a failure, the company was able to identify (a) that it didn't really want to adopt a particularly 'entrepreneurial' mindset or behaviour – except in a very controlled way – and (b) that the earlier problems of stock-outs were not so much caused by a deficiency of risk-taking but by how that specific change had been managed.

During the workshop it transpired that the root cause of the problem lay in staff not being able to adjust quickly enough to a new way of working. Not only had they not got up to speed in their IT skills but also a minority of staff reverted to managing according to the previous style appropriate to their older, less flexible systems.

The Lunarware case underlines the importance of managing change in its totality – not only by thinking through the strategy for the change but also its impact on structure, staff, skills and particularly *style*. It also highlights that change involves abrupt transitions that may disrupt effective performance. In these change traumas it is essential to explore *why* the change appears to be going wrong.

It also emphasizes the need to define 'the problem' thoroughly before devising a solution. In the Lunarware case, the issue appears to have been seized upon, rightly or wrongly, by internal change agents keen on inducing a culture shift. But these same agents lacked sufficient political influence to muster a concentrated attack on the wider problem. Without appropriate positioning as a major intervention, this initiative was bound to fail.

The next exercise helps you to draw out lessons of how change is managed in your business, so that you can begin to reflect directly on whether change is managed well, or not so well.

Exercise 4.4   Managing change in your organization (10 minutes)

List some areas of change in which you are currently involved in the management of your organization. For *one* of these areas of change (preferably a difficult one):

1. What is the *central objective* of the change?
2. What other areas of change does it link into?
3. How thoroughly has the need for change been diagnosed?

4. What are the specific, targeted benefits of this change?
5. Who is in favour of the change, is against it, or is neutral?
6. How is the change positioned in the organization?
7. What level of commitment to the change exists and with whom is it shared?
8. Has adequate time and resources been devoted to making it happen?
9. To what extent is the change being managed as a learning process with the involvement of key stakeholders in the change?

You are very likely to have found from this exercise that the change is being managed in a partly effective way. This is possibly because the process has not been completely thought through, and in some cases the objectives and outputs of the change may also be less than clear.

Improving performance

So far we have focused on strategic learning as applied to more major strategic business development or change issues. But strategic learning is equally applicable to achieving continuous performance improvement within operations. This may involve challenge by both individuals and groups of the efficiency or effectiveness of 'how we do things around here'. This is perhaps best illustrated through two case studies from a health care company.

Case study 4.3(a)   Challenging performance in Globecare

A new MD was appointed from outside to run the international division of a health care company, which we shall call Globecare. The company employed a firm of consultants to help review its international strategy. The scene was the first major meeting between the consulting team and the new MD.

There were three consultants present in addition to the CEO and his finance director. About 25 minutes into the meeting the MD realized that while the consultants' team leader had been involved in the discussions, his two other consultants appeared to be just listening.

Turning to the team leader the MD said: 'Before we go on, may I ask what your two consultants are doing here? They haven't contributed to the meeting at all. I would like both of them to tell me why they are here, and what value they are hoping to add to the meeting.'

'Well, they are ...' began the team leader.

'No, I don't want *you* to tell me why they are here, I want *them* to tell me why they are here.'

Although this interchange might seem somewhat provocative, the MD does seem to have a real point in questioning why the consultants appeared to have come along for the ride.

Case study 4.3(b)   Challenging costs in Globecare

Later that day, the MD and the finance director met privately to discuss areas for possible cost savings in the division. The MD told the finance director of the game-plan:

'I would like to initiate some cost reduction projects. What we should do is to give all our senior managers an individual project to look at *one* area of potential cost savings. We should give them twelve weeks to report back.

'Now, what they will think to themselves is "Thank God that's over – we can carry on as normal". For the next quarter, we will ask them for a progress report and ask each of them for additional cost projects. This will then be part of a continuous management process to reduce costs and become part of the management culture.'

Case study 4.3(a) reveals the MD's habit of challenging areas of waste – whether this is internal or external. In his first meeting with the consultants he did not simply accept their approach, or assume that their *modus operandi* was designed to be effective. He obviously began to conjecture – very quickly in the meeting – that the consultancy time was being ineffectively utilized. His continual sensitivity to 'what is going on' enabled him to make this challenge. No doubt it was also facilitated by thinking back to his prior experiences of consultants elsewhere (and notions of how they operate), which was part of his (personal) recipes.

In Case study 4.3(b) we saw the MD setting up projects to investigate costs. Although not defined as 'learning' projects, these were clearly first attempts to use strategic learning to challenge the status quo. The MD also recognized that he needed to proceed with a degree of stealth and give managers time to get accustomed to challenging existing performance.

4.3   Options for implementing strategic learning

When a significant issue crystallizes within an organization managers are often unclear about the type of process that can be used to address it. This section explores a flexible menu of approaches that can be used to deal with these issues.

This is best explained by considering Figure 4.2, which depicts a cube of choices for strategic learning. The three dimensions that open up are:

1. *Depth*: Does the process aim at covering senior, middle or supervisory levels of management (or a mixture)?
2. *Breadth*: Does it focus on just one functional area, a number of functional areas across the business or does it span business areas (multi-business)?
3. *Duration*: Is the process likely to have a short-, medium- or longer-term

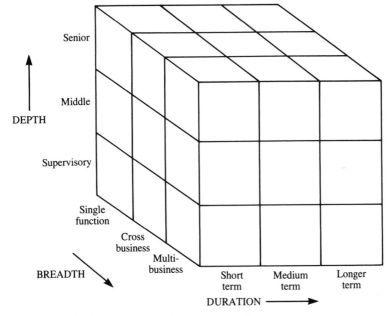

Figure 4.2 Vehicles for strategic learning: the cube

duration? By short-term one might consider a process lasting roughly one or two months; medium-term, three to six months; and longer-term, over six months and possibly (in some instances) up to five years.

The cube highlights the diversity of possible strategic learning vehicles. It also highlights why many initiatives, especially of a tactical nature focusing on short-term training needs, are not too successful.

These initiatives rarely move beyond being at one level (for example, 'supervisory' or 'middle'), are often single functions or at best across a single business unit, and are of shorter-term duration. Exceptions to this might include, for example:

– a quality programme that spans all levels of the organization, across business functions, and is longer term;
– a culture change programme that spans all levels, applies across many businesses, and again is shorter term;
– a change management programme that involves managers across business functions, involves senior and middle levels, and is medium term.

This framework may help managers to map planned initiatives and show how these initiatives might reinforce one another. It may also surface concerns about whether the strategic learning will build up to a critical mass and may show how learning momentum will be sustained over time.

For instance, in the change management programme three issues will require careful consideration:

1. How will supervisory managers become involved?
2. Will the momentum of change be sustained within the business unit if negative influences overspill from other business areas?
3. How will the benefits be reinforced in the longer term?

In the case of the culture change programme, the scale of the intervention is so great that management's commitment may wane before the full effects work through. Finally, in the illustration of the quality programme one might again question whether improvements will be impaired by uneven quality overspilling from other business areas, and also whether the initiative will wane in the long term.

The following case highlights how easy it is to drift into deciding on a particular learning vehicle without fully considering the wider options and their implications.

Case study 4.4 A manufacturing and marketing company – Pulsar

The general manager of a major manufacturing and marketing company, Pulsar Products, decided to involve a larger number of his managers in compiling a strategic plan. Pulsar imported high-value consumer goods and faced fierce competitive pressure to sustain and develop its market position. He asked his human resource manager to 'find out who can facilitate our programme'.

The HR manager telephoned a number of possible suppliers to run a development programme on 'Strategic Planning'. One of these suppliers suggested that a brief visit to find out the client's objectives would be an essential first step – prior to doing a formal proposal.

The HR manager's view was that such a meeting was unnecessary – at least at that stage. All that was required was some idea of what the programme would look like and, of course, what it might cost. He took the view: 'We have told you the levels we want to involve – senior and middle. That should be enough to be going on with.'

If you were the possible supplier what would you do?

As you have been given only a few salient facts, you may well decide that to make a proposal on this basis would be not only risky but inappropriate. Alternatively, you might make some assumptions – for instance, the likely complexity of the strategic analysis, the type of strategic choices that needed to be made, and the extent of implementation issues that might come out.

You might also need to make assumptions about the organization's ability to 'take over the reins' following an initial series of workshops. Indeed, you are obviously being asked to make a lot of assumptions!

Returning to our cube in Figure 4.1, Pulsar's initiative looks very much like one focusing on senior management with possible input by middle levels into the analysis (but perhaps not the choice process). It is also currently seen as a one-off exercise. It thus appears mainly to be focused at a senior level, be cross business and have a short-term horizon.

The programme, however, might need to involve middle managers to a considerably greater extent than currently foreseen. It is also likely to have a longer duration – at minimum be a medium-term activity. It would also require communication of the business strategy at some stage to supervisory levels.

On reflection, what appears to have happened is that the general manager of Pulsar had a sensible idea but passed it over to the 'human resources people' without first thinking it through himself. The HR manager then wondered what to do with it. Rather than push it back upstairs with some possible options, he appears to have decided to cast around for some ideas from possible suppliers, perhaps with a view to doing some do-it-yourself strategic facilitating. Certainly, if an external supplier were used this would serve to legitimize the learning exercise and also to ensure the HR function from retribution if the exercise was perceived not to work. Indeed, in this particular case the idea went into suspension as the HR manager stalled for time, and within weeks the general manager's agenda was overtaken by other events and priorities.

The possible suppliers in such cases are also faced with commercial and ethical dilemmas. Should they, for instance, take the view that this is 'not a viable project' even if it seems profitable? Should they initiate a programme based on the client's espoused requirements in the full knowledge of the possibly severe limitations? Or should they just present a programme that meets the apparent needs with a view to highlighting further requirements at the end of the first stage of the process?

These dilemmas are very real. Some suppliers may take the view that 'we are not there to be the conscience of the client'. However, it may still be prudent to probe, and discover what the problem really is. In the Pulsar case, the cause of the problem is rooted in a few key factors, namely:

- the general manager not thinking through in enough depth not only the content of the issues, the aims and outputs of the exercise, but also the kind of *process* this might entail
- his not being guided as fully as he might in this thinking by in-house professionals
- an initial reluctance to be open with suppliers in order to tap into their experience of the kind of process or vehicle that works/does not work
- fear that the outside supplier might deliberately overscope the project.

The route to strategic learning in this instance appears to demand that all key players – general management, HR adviser, possible external facilitator – be forthright, and investigative, about what they want from the process. Otherwise it is very likely to follow the same unsuccessful path as the Lunarware case mentioned earlier.

4.4 Defining the outputs

Strategic learning is by its very nature a less tangible process. As a result, it can easily become unguided and its effects can become diffuse. In order to focus its application it is therefore essential to target it at specific objectives.

Just as Schaffer and Thomson[1] argue that *change* programmes often fail because they are poorly targeted, so it is even more imperative that strategic learning has explicit goals. This targeting at specific goals can be achieved by examining a number of areas of reinforcing outputs. These are displayed on the matrix in Figure 4.3 as:

– learning
– behaviour
– action.

	STRATEGY	CHANGE	PERFORMANCE IMPROVEMENT
LEARNING	Review of existing strategy	Analysing change issues	Identifying potential for improvement
BEHAVIOUR	Understanding strategic recipes	Developing change capability	Removing blocks to innovation
ACTION	Appraisal of implementation effectiveness	Checking change objectives achieved	Analysing improvements achieved

Figure 4.3   Targeting the outputs from strategic learning (with examples)

In each of the above three cases, outputs may have an impact on either

- strategy
- change
- performance improvement

within the organization.

The grid in Figure 4.3 illustrates the range of possible outputs that can be targeted. We have already considered a number of examples within the strategy/learning box. Moving to the strategy/behaviour box, it may be revealing to analyse the strategic recipes (or what works or doesn't work strategically for the company) at work in your organization. For instance, in the National Health Service (NHS) in the UK, more specialist providers of care now face a challenge to their strategic recipes. In the internal market for services it has become more critical to many purchasers for suppliers to deliver adequate (but not necessarily outstanding) quality of care at low or reasonable cost. The degree to which providers are at the leading edge of technology may thus become less important than in the past. Yet it may be difficult for managers to detach their commitment to older strategic recipes. This reluctance to let go of old recipes may thwart any well-intentioned strategic review (see the strategy/learning box). Organizations facing radical change in their external environment may therefore benefit from including a review of past strategic recipes *explicitly* within the outputs of any strategic review. Ideally this should be conducted *before* the main part of the review in order to surface old recipes.

Moving down further to the strategy/action box, strategic learning can be used to assess the *effectiveness of implementation*. As implementation is often the graveyard of strategy it may be particularly useful to test the effectiveness of implementation using strategic learning.

A key part of effective implementation is that of control. Despite the now burgeoning literature on 'strategic controls' (for example, Goold and Quinn[2]), it would appear that few companies make any practical check to ensure that 'the strategy is on track'. Even where companies make considerable use of strategic *planning* more emphasis is typically placed on financial controls. Where a range of controls are in place, they are often fragmented across a number of functional areas. This makes it difficult to arrive at an overall coherent picture of how implementation of the strategy is proceeding.

With few exceptions (for instance, Kaplan,[3] who describes a more workable control system as being that of the 'balanced score-card'), controls are seen as being at the fringes of strategic management. However, for managers in practice, controls exercise a central role in shaping strategic behaviour, thinking and learning. This is graphically illustrated[4] by instances where controls drive backwards to influence and constrain the style and content of strategic decision-making. Although we normally think of planning as preceding and thus driving controls, the reverse can be the reality.

Although strategic controls appear to be a crucial ingredient of effective strategic management, few companies seem to make them work in practice. Why, if the logic for strategic controls is so strong, do they appear to be underused?

It is possible that strategic controls are difficult to operate because the measurement aspect of controls (often central to rewards and recognition) drives out the learning and feedback process. By routinizing strategic controls managers succeed only in anchoring them to the existing network of control systems. These confirm, rather than challenge, existing views of the business.

Case study 4.5   Strategic controls

In the 1980s, a major chemical group set up a system of strategic controls to supplement its financial measures and to check whether strategy was on course. Progress against key strategic indicators was monitored within each division and by group every year. In addition, major divisions, or those that were undergoing rapid development or where their continuing membership of the Group was subject to debate, were scrutinized on a more frequent and detailed basis.

The framework of strategic controls was found to be an extremely valuable way of checking progress. However, managers had to fight continually against the temptation to make sure that they had 'achieved' milestones.

The above case highlights the need to ensure that managers operate key controls as part of a strategic learning process, rather than as a mechanical reporting routine. Successful strategic controls also require a leadership climate that is conducive to open diagnosis of business issues and makes it feasible to use controls in a genuinely proactive rather than reactive fashion. For instance, in the above case there were two major successes for strategic learning, as the following account illustrates:

1. During *late summer of 1989* some worrying signals of falling demand were detected. This suggested the impending onset of a recession. Divisions were advised by Group to revise their plans to reflect new assumptions about demand and desired capacity levels. Note that this was a full *twelve months prior* to being affected by the recession. Certain other companies, lacking strategic controls, appeared not to have

recognized the recession for one, two or more quarters *after* it was beginning to affect their industry.

2. Subsequently, major areas of the Group began to fall significantly behind performance targets (both external and internal). The Group's share price also came under pressure making the Board concerned about loss of shareholder value. Following a meeting with City advisers, where some creative options were suggested to top management, the chairman decided to initiate a major review of Group strategy and structure.

In the second part of the above account a number of disparate events came together to suggest the need for a new strategy. These events were integrated within the (informal) strategic learning of the directors of the company at the highest level. The decision to embark on a major review of the Group crystallized through a combination of softer initiatives combined with a more formal system of strategic controls or 'triggers'. In this case these triggers served in part as the learning stimulus/vehicle for strategic learning.

We have now discussed three of the boxes in Figure 4.3. Not only can targeted outputs have a direct bearing on the overall strategy (the 'strategy' column), they can also help individuals, teams and departments to manage change (the 'change' column). They may also help achieve major performance improvement (the 'performance improvement' column).

Again, targeted outputs can be separated into learning, behaviour and action. Although these three elements overlap to a degree, it is useful to disaggregate them when targeting strategic learning. For instance, when managing change:

1. The change issues facing a business might be analysed: the objectives of the change, their context, the constraints, together with a strategy for achieving these changes.
2. The change capability of the organization can be analysed to identify those key areas of behaviour that need to be changed, and how this change might be brought about.
3. Finally, for a completed change project, strategic learning can be used to evaluate whether key change objectives have been achieved and at what cost and risk.

In the case of performance improvement, strategic learning can be used to:

- explore the potential for improvement: for instance, by bench-marking with other major organizations, or by assessing how much better competitors are at a key business process, e.g. at customer service;
- focus on removing the blocks to innovation, for example, in terms of

systems, power structure, resource allocation, communication and management structure and style;
– analyse the performance improvements resulting from specific initiatives.

Strategic learning may thus be targeted to cover just some, but not necessarily all, of the nine boxes within the grid of Figure 4.3. Depending upon the specific application, some areas will be of greater importance than others. Figure 4.4 further illustrates how benefits can be targeted using an example from the financial services industry.

In this example, the main focus of strategic learning was in *managing change*. In order to provide an effective vehicle for managing change, however, it also involved delivering a clear idea of how the change plan related to the business strategy. This also had explicit links to cost reduction in terms of specific actions and behavioural style in the organization generally.

In addition to pure learning outputs and an analysis of change issues, the main focus of the entire process was *behaviour/change* – the very centre of the grid. The learning process was therefore highly *emotional* as well as *cerebral*. Further outputs were also targeted through carrying out broader measures of progress against the change plan.

Note that this example was constructed with hindsight. The lesson here is that the targets for strategic learning should be well and explicitly mapped out in advance, not in retrospect.

	STRATEGY	CHANGE	PERFORMANCE IMPROVEMENT
LEARNING	Relating change plan to business strategy	Prioritization of change issues	Defining key areas for improvement
BEHAVIOUR	More focus on cost-led strategy	A more open, flexible style of behaviour	Opening up the flow of ideas
ACTION	Targeting cost reduction	Checking existing progress	Targeting responsiveness/ quality gains

Figure 4.4 Targeting the outputs: example from a financial services company

4.5 Defining the learning process

A variety of vehicles are available for generating strategic learning. These provide a number of ways of injecting vision and constructive challenge into the organization and its sub-units. There is no single, right way of designing a vehicle for strategic learning. Each ingredient has its own advantages and disadvantages, and these vary according to the specific context. In order to focus on a number of key inputs to the learning process let us therefore examine two areas more closely:

- learning workshops
- learning projects.

Learning workshops

Some organizations have never run a genuine strategic workshop. These organizations are typically infested by an overgrowth of committees and by bureaucratic meetings. For such organizations a strategic thought is a rarity; if it ever occurs it is likely to be rapidly smothered by an insidious, creeping tide of meetings to discuss, and then to trivialize.

Case study 4.6 A breath of fresh air within a business school

Academic institutions are not traditionally noted for being visionary, responsive or aware of their external environment and change. To some, the idea of 'customer' is not merely foreign, but alien.

When a business school decided to reflect on its strategy for a key MBA programme, the notion of a 'strategic workshop' as a learning vehicle appeared to be a breath of fresh air – at least compared with our earlier notions of academia.

To prove that business schools can take their own medicine, a small group of enthusiasts met for *one day* to review the strategy for an MBA programme (which we shall call the 'XMBA'). Some market and internal data were available for input and a simple agenda was set along the following lines:

1. Why has the XMBA succeeded in the past? What were its accidental versus sustainable advantages?
2. Where are we now? What is our current market position? How is this changing? What internal issues do we face in sustaining capability, etc.?
3. What options are available for future development?
4. How must we change to sustain our advantage?
5. How will we implement these changes?

Although one day may seem a very short period to do justice to these issues, the short duration for debate had the effect of heightening the feeling of importance of contributions and of the need to make rapid progress.

The workshop had a relatively slow start as different participants struggled to gain control, until at one point one of the key players became restless. He whispered to a colleague, intimating discomfort. His colleague quickly whispered encouragement and without pause the key player rose and took over the role of facilitator.

From that point on the planning process (and outputs) flowed. Within four and a half hours the group of lecturers and XMBA alumni arrived at a number of outputs:

- a distillation of past strategic recipes and an analysis of why the original (largely emergent) strategy had worked
- a clear idea of current competitive position and underlying trends in environmental change
- a number of key internal issues, particularly in how quality could be sustained to support differentiation
- a number of options for expanding the existing programme or extending it into new areas
- a few key areas of change which then required project managing.

Subsequent to the workshop (which proved to be a unanimous success), the team had to work hard (not always successfully) to avoid the 'Everest' syndrome, which is often associated with strategic workshops. This can take the form of:

- having been 'up the mountain' the small team that has had the vision struggles to communicate this to the wider audience in the organization
- owing to sheer exhaustion, the implementation of change becomes a relatively slow process, with the danger that it may become bogged down
- in the rush to get down from the peak to base camp, some of the key aspects of the vision are semi-forgotten or become overlaid with more pressing issues.

Again, this illustration highlights both the power and the potential importance of workshops. In themselves, they are extremely powerful learning vehicles; however, unless the learning is captured, sustained and translated (promptly) into action then the positive effects are quickly diffused.

The advantages of strategic workshops are thus that they:

- time-compress strategic learning by providing managers with a dedicated opportunity to surface and reflect on their issues in joint debate;
- usually highlight key blockages to change in a way which is very difficult to highlight purely through routine management meetings;
- help share the views of different managers, which can often dissolve apparently major differences.

Possible disadvantages of strategic workshops are that they:

- achieve learning breakthroughs that are not then subsequently translated into action;
- create a new form of ritual dissociated and decoupled from day-to-day management reality;
- raise contentious issues that cannot be dealt with by participants because they lack sufficient power or access to power via stakeholders not involved in the workshop.

The last point is well worth amplifying. The initiator is often seeking to generate change, but may not be able to give workshop participants perfect access to the sources of power and influence that are necessary to get full value out of the strategic learning. In some circumstances this can result in a 'learning bomb' effect. While insights build up within the workshop there is (to the participants) no way of releasing this back into the mainstream management process, and the atmosphere within the workshop therefore increases and increases. Skilled facilitation can usually deal successfully with this build-up of tension, but there still needs to be release at some stage.

Obviously, this problem has major implications not merely to workshop programme design and the timely involvement of key stakeholders, but also for anticipating the *outputs* of the strategic learning process. The process of strategic learning, once started, may acquire its own momentum. Yet it would be a foolish designer of the process who would not seek to predict the specific outputs.

Workshops, then, are extremely potent carriers of strategic learning, but they need to be carefully structured (a) in order to reinforce the learning, and (b) to distribute its central outputs into the management process, thereby managing the pressure that might otherwise build up.

Before we leave workshops, let us just consider some of the key questions you need to ask in design:

1. What is the objective of the workshop?
2. How does it relate to other initiatives?
3. What do we see as the key outputs (learning, problem definition, action plans, behavioural shift, etc.) and how will these be documented and communicated and to whom?
4. Who needs to be involved?
5. How will it be positioned in the organization and by whom?
6. Who will facilitate, and are they seen as competent and impartial?
7. Where should it be held and what facilities are required?
8. What are the next steps following the workshop likely to be?
9. What key barriers and blockages may arise and how will these be dealt with and by whom?

10. What specific activities will be undertaken and what inputs will this require?
11. How will these be broken down into discussion groups and who will be in each one?
12. How long is required to make substantial progress on each issue and what happens if tasks are incomplete?

It is essential to consider all these questions at length, rather than rush into a workshop on a particular issue with merely a broad agenda. The questions cover both content *and* process issues, and involve thinking through how these interrelate. They also involve the analysis of both current and future contexts, which provides high-quality feed-in of data and also helps to think through feedback into the management process in detail and in advance.

The second major ingredient of strategic learning is that of projects.

Learning projects

Learning projects are very useful vehicles for capturing strategic learning. These may be conducted by individuals, but are often best tackled by groups of managers. The advantages of learning projects are that they:

- use learning explicitly rather than implicitly in order to analyse key business issues;
- ensure that dedicated time is set aside in order to explore and resolve issues, as time and space provide sufficient reflection to identify a range of options for dealing with these issues;
- encourage managers to target outputs as part of a project process;
- naturally suggest the need to identify and involve stakeholders;
- facilitate subsequent change as the outputs are structured and invariably raise implementation issues.

The possible disadvantages of learning projects (which need managing) include:

- inadequate time being set aside to allow thorough exploration of key issues.
- project management techniques (such as time management, setting milestones, plotting the network of activities and identifying critical paths) being employed partially, or not at all
- the scope of the project being too ill-defined or simply too broad
- managers either seeing the learning project as unreal and possibly trivial (as it is merely a 'learning' project) or, alternatively, as being very real and dangerous, thus driving out the learning.

To be successful, learning projects therefore need to be thoroughly scoped, defined and resourced. They also need to be positioned, not merely within any formal learning programme but also within the core of the organization. This also involves thinking through – in advance – 'what value will the learning project add, where, how and to whom?'.

Examples of learning projects conducted successfully in the past include, among many others:

- acquisition appraisal
- business development opportunity – appraisal and process improvement
- business reappraisal
- communication
- competitive positioning
- competitor intelligence and profiling
- cost management
- customer service and customer care
- distribution channels
- diversification options
- impact of 'green' issues
- investment cases
- IT strategy
- management roles and style
- market resegmentation
- objectives setting
- organisational change
- performance management
- productivity improvement
- simplifying business processes.

The above list highlights the versatility of learning projects, and we shall now explore a series of checklists that learning project teams have found valuable in the past for guiding the course of their projects.

WHAT IS THE SCOPE AND FOCUS OF THE PROJECT?

1. What parts of the organization (vertically and laterally) does the learning project cover, directly and indirectly?
2. What is the specific problem or opportunity upon which it is focused?
3. What underlying causes or factors have conspired to create the problem or opportunity?
4. Who owns the problem (or opportunity)?

WHAT KEY ISSUES IS IT LIKELY TO INVOLVE?

1. What strategic issues are involved?
2. What operational issues are involved?
3. What financial issues are likely to have an impact?
4. What organizational and behavioural issues have a bearing?
5. How should it be positioned in the organisation and by whom?

WHAT ARE OUR DESIRED OUTPUTS?

1. What key areas of *ambiguity* do we wish to remove?
2. What specific *options* do we want to generate?
3. What kinds of *decision* do we expect to emerge?
4. What *plans* for *improving performance* are we seeking to deliver?
5. What insights on *implementation* do we wish to secure, particularly on any *barriers to change*?
6. What *beliefs, attitudes* and *behaviours* are we seeking to shift?
7. In what areas do we want to strengthen our coherence as a *team*?
8. What specific *learning gaps* do we want to fill and which *skills* do we want to develop?

HOW WILL WE GET THESE OUTPUTS AND WHAT INPUTS ARE NEEDED?

1. How long do we need for the learning project?
2. How long do we have?
3. What resources (people, skills, knowledge, information) do we have and what do we require?
4. What short-cuts are available (for instance, using ready-to-hand data)?
5. Who can be recruited to help us with the task, or to secure necessary resources?
6. What key tasks and sub-tasks does the learning project break down into?
7. Who will do which tasks (and do they have the proper skills)?
8. What milestones do we need to set to monitor progress?
9. What interim outputs should we agree to deliver, to help pull the project forward?
10. What key activities are on our critical path?
11. How will we ensure that all members of the team participate in sufficient depth?
12. Who will coordinate the project and how will it be facilitated?

WHAT OPTIONS ARE AVAILABLE FOR RESOLVING KEY ISSUES?

1. What key options exist that are both obvious and less obvious and how should they be appraised?
2. How attractive are these options in terms of:
   (a) likely benefits and costs?
   (b) risks?
   (c) implementation effort and pain?
3. From this analysis, how might these options be reshaped to become more attractive and feasible?

WHAT WIDER ISSUES ARE RAISED BY THE LEARNING PROJECT?

1. What light has the learning project shed on other areas of strategic development or organizational change?
2. What does it suggest about underlying organizational learning?
3. What future lessons for applying strategic learning in the organization have been generated?

WHAT SHOULD WE PRESENT AND WHY?

1. What was the project all about (in brief) and why did it appear worth undertaking?
2. What are the key outputs of the project?
3. What wider lessons have emerged?
4. What areas of implementation should now move forward and what will help or hinder success?
5. What issues still remain as unresolved and how should these be tackled?

HOW SHOULD IT BE PRESENTED, TO WHOM, AND BY WHOM?

1. How should the project outputs be communicated given their sensitivity, balanced against the need to challenge or reshape existing perspectives?
2. How can recipients' objections be anticipated in advance?
3. How can likely resistance be minimized through appealing to their concerns, agendas and values?
4. How can outputs be documented without weighing the learning project down in unnecessary paperwork so that insights are lost?
5. Who (among project stakeholders) should be invited to take ownership of outputs?
6. Who should be presented as having contributed to and having ownership of the project outputs?

Learning projects can play an extremely valuable role in strategic learning, either as stand-alone projects or as sets of interrelated projects.

My message to those concerned that these projects are sensitive and 'high risk' is the same as the advice I gave to a major IT company recently in a London pub, as my back was being warmed by a (too hot) log fire:

> Learning projects are actually low risk because they involve fully mobilizing the learning potential of groups. Conventional, stand-alone management programmes which use live issues as learning material are often higher risk as there is often nowhere for the learning outputs to go. If you are using live ammunition, it is much safer to shoot it at outdoor targets than believe you can practise safely indoors.

4.6 Moving into action

This chapter has covered a variety of approaches to devising vehicles for strategic learning. It now concludes with a final exercise aimed at devising a prototype for strategic learning in your business.

Exercise 4.5 Your business (10 minutes)

Using the frameworks explored in this chapter:

1. Identify *one* issue that might form the basis of a strategic learning exercise in your organization.
2. What combination of strategic workshop(s)/learning projects seem best suited to deliver this need?
3. What key outputs would you hope to deliver?
4. Who should facilitate it?
5. How should this be best launched and positioned in the organization?

We are now ready to consider the core case studies, which I hope amply demonstrate the value to be harvested from strategic learning.

References

1. Schaffer, R. H. and Thomson, H. A., 'Successful change programs begin with results', *Harvard Business Review*, January–February 1992, pp. 80–9.
2. Goold, M. and Quinn, J. J., *Strategic Control*, The Economist Books, 1990.
3. Kaplan, R. S. and Norton, D. P., 'The balanced scorecard – measures that drive performance', *Harvard Business Review*, January–February 1992, pp. 71–9.
4. Grundy, A. N., *Corporate Strategy and Financial Decisions*, Kogan Page, 1992.

5

When learning drives strategic decisions: the Dowty experience

5.1 Decision-making: the imperative

Increasingly, learning is being seen as an integral part of the strategic decision-making process. During a major review of the strategy of a telecommunications and information systems business, learning was pivotal in crystallizing a number of key decisions.

Although some of the lessons from this experience have been described elsewhere,[1] these were very much distilled from a *planning* and *change* perspective primarily. In this chapter we are able to take a *learning* perspective, which highlights some new and interesting insights on strategic learning from this case.

The case described is that of Dowty Communications. During the time of the review the company had a turnover of approximately £120 million. It had significant operations in half a dozen countries; small businesses in a number of others; and possible areas for development in a number of others. The case study is described as follows:

- Brief overview: background to the strategic review
- Summary of the review as a learning process
- Key learning outputs
- What was learned about the strategic learning process
- Reflections and conclusions.

The core section in this account is: 'What was learned about the learning process?' Although the other outputs are important – for instance, the 'key learning outputs' – in some ways what was learned about the learning process is more interesting. This tells us much about how strategic learning can be orchestrated, and demonstrates the great value of strategic learning when the correct process has been implemented.

The case is based on the reflections (three years later) of the external consultant (the author) and of two of the then directors of Dowty Communications. These reflections were captured at a number of informal meetings.

5.2 Brief overview: background to the strategic review

Business history

During the early 1980s, Dowty Communications (formerly CASE Communications) was a rapidly growing, entrepreneurial company based at Watford, England. It achieved major and early successes with wide area networks (WAN) and had built a solid market position in the UK. Its success was based on speed and flexibility, with the company having a relatively flat structure – until the mid/late 1980s.

During the mid-1980s the company grew by spreading its business activities in a number of ways, for instance:

- *geographically*: in Europe, the US and elsewhere
- *product range*: through developing its service business and also seeking to develop local area network (LAN) products
- *distribution channels*: developing a range of direct and indirect channels to market.

The company thus became increasingly more complex. As it grew, there were also some major setbacks – for instance, in one major overseas subsidiary significant losses occurred, resulting in withdrawal. In the UK there was also a significant pause in market demand following earlier growth spurts.

The company then needed refinancing and was taken over by Dowty Group in the late 1980s, although it retained the CASE name until 1991.

Planning history

Although there had been several attempts to use planning as a learning vehicle prior to 1990/91, these had not proved to be particularly successful. Indeed, it would be fair to say that prior to 1990 the company relied on more basic planning and control routines (and would thus be in the 'planning' phase at the far left of Figures 3.2 and 3.3 in Chapter 3).

In early 1990 a number of issues and agendas conspired to crystallize a major attempt at strategic learning for this important part of Dowty's IT Division. These issues and agendas included:

1. The need for the various businesses to deliver the aspirations of Dowty Group following the immediate post-acquisition period.
2. The problem faced by the (new) MD and his team on a daily basis of sorting out which new business ideas to back, and which to exclude. As the MD is reported to have said at the time: 'I get at least one new business idea every day across my desk. We obviously can't do everything. But how do we justify our decisions?'
3. There was encouragement from Group for the MD to complete one 'breakthrough' project in 1990. This practice had become very popular and important in the Group as a means of seeking a quantum, as opposed to merely continuous performance improvement. Conducting a strategy review would help not only the top team deal with its medium- and longer-term aspirations but would also fulfil the need to complete a breakthrough project.
4. Once the idea of a strategic review was born, this cascaded rapidly down into the personal agendas of at least one of the directors of Dowty Communications. In particular, the newly appointed director of business development, Dave King, was given the task of co-ordinating the strategic review. As one of his personal objectives, this was on his critical path in fulfilling his (new) job role. This put Dave under significant pressure to 'deliver a strategic plan' by a date in the early autumn.

This leads us to the learning process that underpinned the strategic review.

5.3 The review as a learning process

The progress of the review breaks into three major stages[2]:

- analysis
- choice
- implementation.

The key learning outputs phase-by-phase are dealt with in Section 5.4, but we first need to address the overall learning process.

Overlap in the three stages

Although conventional texts on strategy often show these three stages as discrete, this was not found to be the case during the Dowty review. A more realistic view of the process is depicted in Figure 5.1. This highlights that the

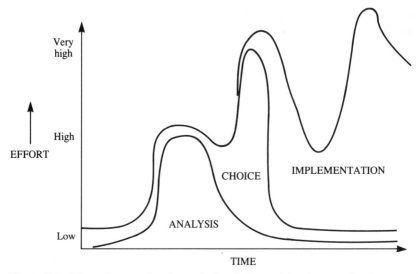

Figure 5.1 Managing overlap in analysis, choice and implementation in strategic reviews

analysis typically crystallizes options and, in some cases, decisions through the analysis process. In the 'choice' phase several decisions that have already emerged are merely approved. The main process in formalizing these decisions is thus more of a *political* nature rather than one involving careful, rational deliberation from first principles.

The other area to highlight is that choice is an important element shaping the analysis phase. Again, many strategy textbooks describe analysis as a very logical process, but what you choose to analyse can play an important role in shaping the analysis and subsequent choices. For instance, in Dowty Communications the main focus of analysis (which we shall see later) was on product/market development – and even then, principally market development. There was much less emphasis on technology and capability development. Although both of these issues did have some dedicated learning workshops, they did not emerge until later as being central to strategic development. Fortunately, at a later stage these issues did emerge as important, the learning insights were suitably amplified, and thus the review was able to be extended. This explains why some 'choice' is shown as occurring in parallel with the early analysis phase.

Also, the 'analysis' phase is rarely closed down. Invariably, there will be areas of further investigation, particularly at the fringe of the core business strategy. The fact that 'the strategy' has not then been totally delivered as a nice, neat package may give rise to some management discomfort. Yet it is normal and natural that there should be further areas to explore and evaluate. There are also continuing choices during the implementation phase, and an ongoing need for further analysis.

Further, some preparation for implementation needs to 'precede' the actual implementation. Also, the strategy needs to be evaluated in terms of 'how difficult will this be (potentially) to implement?'. Although to some degree that actually happened during this review, the extent to which it did so was not large. Subsequently, this caused problems in paving the way for implementation, and in putting forward too big a task of development and change – all at the same time.

My own reflections (captured in Tring, Hertfordshire, May 1993) are as follows:

> The trouble was that the implementation tasks were fundamentally bigger and more complex than the task of strategic analysis – which I believe we could perhaps have simplified a bit. I just wonder whether a lot of what went wrong was that the problem of gaining complete commitment to the strategy was never fully resolved, although it is fair to say that this was severely aggravated by external circumstances.

Issues, tasks and levels of involvement

Figure 5.2 (see also Figures 5.3 and 5.4 for other levels of involvement) shows the matrix of key issues that were dealt with through the learning process. This highlights the extent of involvement at key levels of management, and also of the small team of core facilitators: Dave King (internally) and myself (externally).

Figure 5.2 shows that although the middle managers had a very substantial involvement in the learning process, they did not have any real involvement directly in the choice phase. With hindsight, this phase might have been performed differently. Once the top team had crystallized the strategic decisions that it felt were appropriate, it might well have been beneficial to:

- recheck the strategic logic of these decisions with selective members of middle management
- get a more realistic feel for the implementation task.

This would not only have checked out the basis for the decisions, but would also have paved the way for implementing necessary change.

Also, the involvement of the top team was mainly focused on the choice phase. Although each of the directors was charged with sponsoring one key strategic analysis task, this fell far short of giving each of them a broader

	Involvement Levels		
	Top Team	Facilitator Group	Middle Managers
ANALYSIS June–August 1990	SWOT analysis Mission/ goals Individual to middle manager teams	Tested SWOT analysis Distilled key strategic issues Analysed macro-options	Market potential Country analysis Technology appraisal Business processes People capability
CHOICE September 1990	Country decisions Channel decisions Product decisions	Documenting rationale	No involvement (directly)
IMPLEMEN-TATION December 1990	Individuals to lead projects	Project management process	Workshops on managing change Possible involvement in projects

Figure 5.2   Key learning activities during the review

picture of the emerging lessons. Instead, these choices were stored up for a 'big bang' workshop scheduled to last two days. (This, in fact, went into an extended session of over five days because of the number, complexity and political sensitivity of the decisions under consideration.)

Managing the transition into implementation

The other key feature of the process was that implementation was seen by some players as just something that would 'drop out of the plan'. In the past, the business plan had principally documented the operational actions required to deliver short-term performance. Although the strategic review involved a much longer and bolder exploration of the external and internal issues, long and short term, it was still expected that budgets would simply 'fall out' of the strategic plan.

This highlights an apparent difference of views that emerged between the facilitator team and the rest of the top team. According to Dave King:

> It just needed someone to use it as a big lever to make the change. Many people sensed the need to change.

But what appeared to be happening was that:

> We [the facilitators] did get too close to it at times. We really became well ahead of the others in our thinking, there was the problem of catch-up.

This may account for some of the learning droop that occurred during the transition to implementation mode (see Figures 5.3 and 5.4 on pages 110 and 111). Although the pair of facilitators provided a project management process and further learning frameworks to steer implementation, these efforts typically petered out. Also, a number of managing change workshops were organized by the then director of personnel, Nicky Burton, who became closely involved with the facilitator team as the review progressed.

Although these managing change workshops were successful, the learning outputs relating to implementation were once again mainly sealed up inside the workshops and were not fully released to steer the process of implementing change. This was mainly a result of delay in communicating the strategy which was in turn frustrated by developments at Dowty Group level. Nicky Burton reflects:

> The communication of the strategy was planned to coincide with the middle management development workshops. This was frustrated because of a pending requirement at Group to make substantial cost savings.
> The scene had changed politically very quickly. A learning point was that when you follow an intensive strategic review process this scene is in substantial flux. Timing is thus critical – what seemed like good timing, suddenly now wasn't. ...

Although there were many organizational distractions at that time – for example, a pending recession, the impact of defence cuts on Dowty Group etc. – this still does not account for all of the learning droop. This topic is dealt with at greater length in Section 5.5.

5.4 Key learning outputs

The key learning outputs of the strategic learning process can be readily summarized, dealing with each major stage in turn.

Initial learning lessons

ANALYSIS

1. The company's markets were becoming less attractive owing to their greater maturity, competitive rivalry and increased investment requirements.

2. The company's competitive position was not as strong as had previously been believed. In a number of areas it had a competitive disadvantage (echoing Chapter 3).
3. The range of business areas had become very complex and in many areas the company lacked critical mass.
4. A relatively small number of core activities accounted for almost all the business profit stream.
5. There were symptoms of a backlog of undigested strategic change that had accumulated throughout the 1980s.

CHOICE

1. The company needed to narrow its range of activities.
2. Any new activities would need to be carefully screened against the existing strategies and against new business criteria.
3. Some significant operational changes needed to be made in the UK.

IMPLEMENTATION

1. The backlog of change was considerable and presented an even greater challenge than the earlier analysis and choice phases.

Given the nature of these difficulties I believe that it was inevitable (with hindsight) for the review to have become (temporarily) suspended in late 1990 and early 1991.

Dave King neatly summarizes the problem of making the transition into implementation thus:

> I really don't know what we could have done to better manage the links to implementation. I mean, obviously we should have rolled out the communication. But, to avoid the strategic exhaustion, perhaps we should have given them all some sort of holiday; who knows, a strategic holiday. But would anything have happened then?

Reflecting on the above, it is apparent that much of the benefit of strategic learning came through managers changing their views of the organization and its environment. This involved:

- managers realizing that they didn't know some of the things they thought they knew
- managers discarding assumptions about the business that had been taken for granted
- managers discovering that their assumption that other managers held the same or similar views was incorrect

– managers realizing, for the first time, that their underlying assumptions on the position and direction of other business units had caused considerable and unncessary disputes and contention that could now, in many instances, be dissolved.

Once managers have collectively moved through this thought process in unison, it is often difficult for them to imagine their old way of looking at things, which now seems simplistic. However, there may be a time lag before the new set of strategic perspectives fully engages behaviour and action. As Nicky Burton reflects:

> The strategic planning became the 'unfreezing' process, although whether we all saw it like that at the time, I'm not really sure.

The above points are now overlaid by the further lessons which, with hindsight, either were or might have been learned.

Further learning lessons

ANALYSIS

1. The resources needed to develop the local area network (LAN) business and international business were probably much greater than the initial analysis suggested (relative to both before the strategic review and, to a lesser extent, after it).
2. The company's internal business processes and structure required *considerable* redesign and simplification, rather than just continuous improvement.

CHOICE

1. Some decisions to put on 'hold' involvement in countries where there was marginal advantage were probably unwise. This sustained an excessively wide spread of activities given the resource base available to International.
2. The decision to adopt a low-cost strategy in some product areas was not sufficiently targeted at levels that would actually be *lowest* cost – for both present *and future*.
3. The onset of the economic recession in late 1990 meant that the company needed to scale down its strategic commitments rather than letting the strategy and its financial projections become less relevant. Nicky Burton adds to this:

But the strategy did give us a set of criteria to choose what we would keep, reduce or abandon, and the strategy remained highly relevant in how the downsizing decisions were made.

4. The process rules that were put in place for the top team's workshops turned out to be indispensable. This included, for instance, putting on the wall of the workshop room a list of P's – forbidden behaviours – for instance, being political, picky, procrastinating, etc. Dave King reflects that:

> The process rules really worked. I mean, could you have seen X and Y (two directors) saying the things that they did say without that?

IMPLEMENTATION

1. The issue of culture change, or more specifically shift in management style, although difficult to address was a key one for successful implementation. This required adjustment to different business performance reviews and controls, to new approaches in rewards and recognition and to decision processes. The opportunistic style with which middle managers approached new business opportunities needed to become more channelled but not made so rigid as to drive out entrepreneurial behaviour. This needed to be reflected in clear role examples from the top team.

2. The top team began to learn that during implementation they needed to partially 'let go' by sharing the tasks with middle managers. This might have also involved appointing key middle managers (and not themselves directly) to project manage change, although Nicky Burton looks backs on this in a slightly different way:

> I don't know whether there were the skills to do this across the board. No, I think there weren't.

Extending strategic learning to corporate level

I believe that some of these learning lessons were realized by the management team at the time, and some with hindsight. Looking back I still feel personally that the management team might have achieved earlier and closer interfaces with Dowty Group management in order to share some of their insights rather than store these up for the end product. For instance, Dave King reflects:

> The really big mistake was not actually getting Group somehow involved. Perhaps we could have had one or two people down to see what was going on. I don't know. But the message we did get was that they thought very differently to us.

Nicky Burton adds:

> Yes, I agree, indeed they [Group] thought differently all along on a whole range of issues.

Closer interfaces with Group might have ensured not merely an early interface with Dowty Group managers' perspectives – thus linking into *corporate learning* – but also beginning to feed into and off the corporate agenda. If this had been put in place then the problem of inability to gain sufficient investment of Group for the strategy in late 1990/early 1991, would have been highlighted sooner. However, Nicky Burton's comments show that the differing mindsets between Group and Division made the gap in thinking appear too difficult to bridge through a shared learning exercise.

Once again this highlights the problem of extending the learning into wider parts of the organization. Here there is always a dilemma: if you try to do this you may find your more local learning crushed by agendas elsewhere; yet if you don't do it, the strategic learning is completed and then becomes difficult to adapt to meet these agendas. The problem, of course, becomes less severe if these agendas can be explored in advance – assuming that senior management is well networked *and*, more importantly, are prepared to be open about what they sense is happening elsewhere.

5.5   What was learned about the learning process?

The Dowty Communications case is rich in lessons about the strategic learning process. These lessons have been further distilled into the following points, which are explored in turn:

- Infuse the learning within the organization
- Make decision-making an explicit learning process
- Manage personal and corporate agendas effectively
- Define 'the givens' to stabilize the process
- Loosen control to spread the learning process beyond the top team
- Build learning into 'how we do things around here'
- Avoid overdosing and manage the 'come-down'
- Strategic learning may well shift the existing power base
- Involve the leader at the centre of the process and build his or her learning capability
- Inject learning into implementation
- Use communication as a vehicle for learning
- The successful facilitator must be an excellent learner.

Infuse the learning within the organization

Unless strategic learning is infused within and across the organization its impact will be rapidly blunted. In the Dowty case this blunting occurred for the following reasons:

1. Senior management were involved initially during the early analysis but then to no particularly great extent until the 'choice' phase. Equally, middle managers were involved heavily during the analysis phase but were substantially excluded from the choice phase, and then expected to remobilize in implementation. This all encourages unlearning.
2. Group management were excluded from the learning so that business-level learning did not interface with corporate learning.

The effect of point (1) above is graphically illustrated in Figures 5.3 and 5.4, which show the roller-coaster of involvement levels of service and middle management. Notice both the blips of involvement, how they occur at different times for senior versus middle management, and also the loss of momentum and delay prior to communicating the strategy. These curves were drawn after the event. I would advise anyone planning a major strategic learning exercise to sketch these in advance during their planning process!

The end product in terms of organization learning is described by Dave King:

> Yes, I am sure that very many people learned an awful lot about the organization at middle levels, especially through the workshops helping them manage change issues. In fact, they [the insights] were real, positively dangerously real at times.

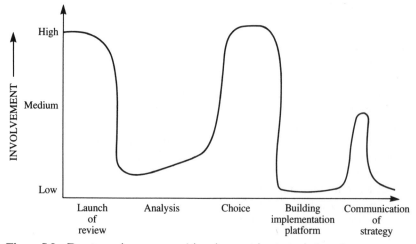

Figure 5.3 Dowty senior managers' involvement in strategic learning

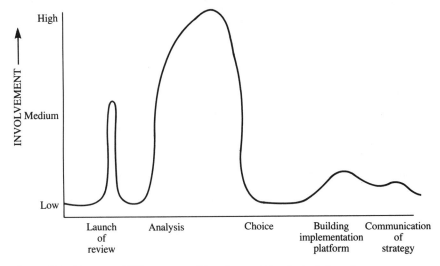

Figure 5.4   Dowty middle managers' involvement in strategic learning

Make decision-making an explicit learning process

The Dowty managers were focused primarily on delivering a tangible output – the strategic plan – rather than on achieving strategic insights, *per se*. This meant that once they had delivered the outputs from the strategic analysis, made some key strategic decisions, and determined what resources should be allocated, they felt their task was substantially complete. These outputs included:

- mission and longer-term goals (profitability and growth)
- product/market strategies to achieve these goals and necessary technological development
- choices (differing between business units) of generic strategies and bases for sustaining competitive advantage
- specific plans to develop rapidly, hold or divest
- areas for quantum improvement in internal capability – processes, people, systems and style.

Yet the 'strategic plan', which ran to more than 50 pages (reflecting the complexity of the business and the need to explain and justify the decisions), contained a number of outstanding issues, for instance:

1. Some of the country strategies needed more refinement: more analysis was required.

2. The issue of how to respond to one-off but larger prospects outside the core countries was still unresolved.
3. Further work was needed to develop a coherent strategy for the service business.
4. Further work was needed to explore how more, and larger, customers (and larger contracts) could be secured to shift the mix of business.

This suggests that a strategic review may deliver a range of outputs besides the core strategy. Outputs include specific decisions, areas for change, new strategic issues (to be resolved) and further specific areas for business development. This is depicted in Figure 5.5.

Our account therefore indicates:

1. While a core of outputs – 'the strategy' – can be fixed, other areas can be fluid, including business development opportunities, the impact of ongoing change and new or outstanding strategic issues.
2. In addition, some areas may be semi-fluid, including strategic criteria

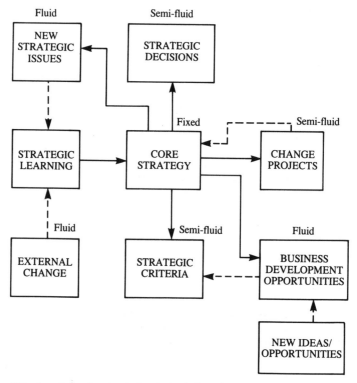

Figure 5.5   Inputs and outputs to strategic learning

(which may require amending as more is learned about the opportunity stream) and also certain strategic decisions (which may require more refinement). Also, some of the change projects may be semi-fluid. These may also reshape the core strategy – for instance, if they assume more time or resources than was envisaged, or if it becomes apparent that the organization's capability to implement the strategy is not strong.

Figure 5.5 helps resolve, at a practical level, some of the conflict we saw earlier, in Chapter 3, between the design versus emergent schools of strategy. Depending upon the nature of the external environment and preferred management style, the size and relative influence of the core processes in Figure 5.5 will differ. But doing a 'strategic plan' does not preclude fluidity: indeed, it provides a basis, some framework for flexibility. It also provides a focus for further strategic learning.

Manage personal and corporate agendas effectively

During the strategic review, a number of personal agendas needed to be managed, for example:

1. The MD came under pressure from Group to institute a reorganization which, in the course of time, would help reduce costs. He was therefore faced with wanting to deliver the strategic review (a) as this was started, (b) to help refocus the business and, (c) to satisfy Group's requirements. While the reorganization fitted well with the *content* of the change, its incidence was likely to upset the decision-making and implementation processes.

    As Dave King elaborated:

    > Our MD, he was trying to do a lot, many things with the strategic review. I think probably too much. For instance, you could see him trying to do team building, for example at the strategic meetings. . . .

2. At times the choice phase seemed to be derailed as different senior managers sought to put on to the shared agenda some of the issues that they desperately wanted to resolve. For instance, specific issues such as (a) salesforce effectiveness or (b) weak business performance in particular areas seemed to take up more time than was available. This highlights a tension between what the facilitators were trying to achieve and some specifics that key players were (understandably) trying to include. With hindsight, these issues could have been channelled more forcibly into 'implementation activities', but perhaps key stakeholders felt that these issues would otherwise have been swept aside.

3. The official agenda of the team of facilitators was to deliver the strategic plan and to devise detailed business plans. It was not explicitly concerned with implementation. However, it emerged that the scale of the changes involved to secure effective implementation was so great that these agendas had to change. If, for instance, Figures 5.3 and 5.4 were extended into the implementation phase (as they might have been) we would have seen an involvement of both senior and middle managers coming back at least to medium levels. This posed particular dilemmas for the external facilitator (myself) as to when and how to highlight this as it might well have been construed as 'an attempt to print consulting fees'. Also, Dave King, the internal facilitator, might have been viewed as seeking to perpetuate his strategic role, which had obviously given him significantly greater prominence and influence – at least during the peak of the review. This was not, however, without personal risk, as he explains:

> At the time, I hadn't appreciated just how high risk it was. Looking back, it was relatively obvious.

The agendas of key individuals (real or imagined) must therefore be recognized if they are not to distort the process of strategic learning.

Define the 'givens' to stabilize the process

During the strategic learning review, the 'givens' may well change as the review progresses. For instance, at the early phases there may be relatively low 'givens' except some notion of the 'range of business we are in' – possibly a draft (but not final) mission statement and a tentative (but not rigid) view of financial objectives and constraints.

During the choice phase managers are well advised to tackle those areas for decision that are either very central or likely to be less contentious, or both. This enables them to feel that good progress has been made, thereby securing a base for further learning. It also provides them with more 'givens'. This is not unlike taking an examination: it is advisable to tackle some of the easier issues first.

Subsequently, further 'givens' may crystallize. For instance, the core strategy and strategic criteria may spell out the business areas that will definitely *not* be considered for further development. For instance, this may involve areas that are:

- in countries/geographic areas that have been excluded
- market segments, distribution channels and (possibly) entire markets that are not seen as attractive or longer term

- types of acquisition or similar deals in which the company does not want to become involved
- products or technologies that are beyond the company's potential to gain competitive advantage
- business opportunities that are simply too small, too complex, or too difficult to implement or opportunities that are too big, resource hungry or risky.

Strategic learning, therefore, does not need to be infinitely wide-ranging, but it does need to be carefully telescoped, and great care should be taken when thinking through the 'strategic' don'ts'.

Loosen control to spread the learning process beyond the top team

The Dowty case represents a major attempt to involve all the senior and middle managers of an organization in learning about its future direction. However, the senior team could not easily relinquish some of the control at the beginning of the implementation process, even though all of its middle managers had gone through a three-day managing change workshop programme (five of these were run in total).

Although this may be a simple thing to point out, letting go is much harder than it may seem, as it may entail a significant shift in management style alongside confidence in capability at middle levels.

Build learning into 'how we do things around here'

During the course of the strategic review, a number of learning routines were created but were not subsequently incorporated fully into routines. These included:

1. *Strategic workshops*: these were seen to be related to the review itself rather than as a central vehicle for implementing cross-functional change.
2. *Customer views*: these had been elicited from the organization and found to be extremely useful, but were not built into a regular or period monitoring process.
3. *Business measures*: although an attempt was made to set up a balanced set of controls or 'key business resources' to track the strategy, reviews of progress were not formally built into management's agenda.
4. *Cost reduction/simplification*: a project to simplify product design and reduce costs was begun, but this was not then backed up by benchmarking from similar industries.
5. *Learning spin-offs*: a number of additional issues came out of the middle

management strategic change workshops. Some of these managers offered to pursue issues such as learning projects, but gained little solid support for this in the organization.

6. *Competitor analysis*: this proved to be a great stimulus to the learning process throughout, but no provision was made to continue this even though a competitor/customer database was at the design stage.

7. *Market/competitive analysis*: another database was created for all the company's products/markets. Although there were many gaps in the data, there was no real push to fill out the analysis, even where this was needed to think through in more detail the strategy development.

The key lesson here is to avoid a surge or tide of strategic learning that is then followed by the tide going completely out, which links into our next point.

Avoid overdosing and manage the 'come-down'

Strategic learning can be an exciting and intoxicating experience. It can also be very tiring as it is strenuous to keep in double-loop learning mode for a sustained period of time. This means that managers need to pace themselves, and it also highlights the need to make the learning process design no more complex than necessary. Possibly the *analysis phase* at Dowty might have been slightly simplified, but, given the backlog of strategic indigestion, one doubts that this could have been reduced, for instance, by a factor of 0.5. Dave King explains this graphically:

> What we should definitely *not* have done is to hit them [senior management] with a change process which again looked complex. With hindsight, I can just see them switching off.

The danger is that, with the core of learning completed, managers step back into single-loop learning. But continued reflection and iteration may be required well into the implementation process.

This problem is akin to that of mobilizing an army for battle. Once this is achieved and the battle fought, the troops may want to demobilize rather than maintain a war footing. Once demobilized, it becomes difficult to remobilize, except for minor exercises.

Strategic learning may well shift the existing power base

During the review, the influence of key players in the management team shifted as a result of their involvement. This indicates that learning is not a power-neutral process. Dave King illustrates this in looking at how the review was used within the top team and at middle levels:

What you may have a problem with, is when you set something up trying to involve people...when in fact you (or others) really believe there is a need to drive some particular things through.

Not only does being central in the learning process help to position players in the management team, but it also gives them greater power through the wealth of information gained. Although this is typically well shared within the team, the internal facilitator and those with heavy involvement in key projects may possess some advantage as a result.

The external facilitator may acquire some influence in shaping events. He or she must be especially careful of being perceived to 'take sides' on contentious issues without objective justification.

Involve the leader at the centre of the process and build his or her learning capability

Although it is a truism that the leader must be involved in a symbolic way and as a key stakeholder in a strategic review, making this happen is not always easy. Not only are there likely to be many other distractions for the MD/CEO, but there are a number of factors that may actively discourage a sufficiently deep involvement:

1. The leader may feel that, having appointed an internal (and external) facilitator, he or she should not require a regular, detailed involvement in the programme.
2. By becoming too involved and, possibly, holding up the process, the leader may not want to be used as an excuse for 'why we didn't deliver the plan on time'.
3. There may be (possibly valid) reasons for not getting too close to the project – making it harder to be objective in the 'choice phase'.
4. The leader may feel increasingly uncomfortable about the process. Rather than become more involved, this may actually invite *less* involvement, which, in turn, may heighten discomfort as uncertainty grows.
5. There may be valid concerns about not wanting to foreclose options prior to the choice phase.
6. The leader may feel reluctant to admit that he or she is learning as the process proceeds, especially where strategic analysis or other tools are being utilized in which he or she is not fluent.

These factors may compound with others (such as 'I am simply too busy anyway') to result in effective decoupling of the leader from the learning process.

To remedy this possible problem, the facilitators should hold weekly or fortnightly debriefing sessions with the MD. They might also use these sessions not just to explore interim outputs but also to explain the process and tools – to share the learning process. This also helps build ownership so that the MD does not just see the process as a 'nice-to-do' but as one that needs building into organizational routines.

Inject learning into implementation

This is a point that we have covered already, but is nevertheless most important. The following are examples of strategic learning injected into implementation:

1. Change projects should be linked to the strategic plan via their strategic objectives.
2. Further insights should be gained about the external environment and about internal capability as the projects progress.
3. Continually think of ways of accelerating progress across the change front as a whole, for instance, either by combining specific change projects or by engaging them in a convoy.
4. Be alert to instances where an area of change turns out to be more complex or difficult, or of longer duration, than was thought originally. This may require procuring additional or different resources, or splitting the project into more than one unit. Ultimately, this may also impact on the overall critical path for organizational change.

Use communication as a vehicle for learning

In the Dowty case, a major opportunity was missed by not inviting managers' input to the *implementation requirements* of the strategy where the strategy itself was communicated.

Again, communication in organizations can be a two-way interchange, yet in this instance the process was seen as cascading down rather than two-way and iterative. Besides getting a clearer view of implementation issues, managers can also gain much greater ownership of the strategy.

The successful facilitator must be an excellent learner

The facilitators need to be excellent learners to be effective.

1. A facilitator should have patience in debating the process to make sure it is not 'just about right' but that it is 'absolutely right'.

2. The internal facilitator should have the ability to remain unswayed by personal views or pet ideas. Only then can he or she challenge groupthink. He or she also needs to be able to use strategic frameworks, but be mindful of the need to filter these to avoid indigestion.
3. The external facilitator should have the ability to learn very rapidly about the organization. He or she needs to have a broad knowledge of the management disciplines concerned with 'soft' as well as 'hard' issues. Also, the ability to filter recipes of 'what has worked elsewhere' to the new context is essential. Finally, he or she needs to be sufficiently flexible to blend with the needs of the management team but should also be able – when the time is right – to challenge core assumptions.

This means that the facilitators need to work hard to sustain their own learning. I personally learned a great deal from involvement in the Dowty strategic review – not just at the time, but also through subsequent reflection.

5.6 Reflections and conclusions

Dowty Communications thus yields a wealth of insights about strategic learning. This major experiment yielded results which, at the time, caught the attention and imagination of managers throughout the organization. I believe it also helped initiate a process of change that was of great longer-term value despite the early frustrations and setbacks. We have also been able to draw perhaps some even more important lessons from this: on the strategic learning process itself.

During the case the issue of using strategic learning to drive implementation became a recurrent theme. This theme is now much amplified by a case from a non-competing company in another part of the same industry – Mercury Communications.

We leave this case by summarizing some *do's* and *don'ts* of strategic learning which distil the key lessons of this case.

Key do's and don'ts of strategic learning

LEARNING DO'S

1. Set and continually reinforce expectations about how and when the process will become difficult.
2. Break-down the analysis phase into manageable parts with very clear objectives and ensure that these are met *with least effort*.

3. Try to involve Group or other external stakeholders at key stages rather than take the apparently easier route of going it alone.
4. Give debriefings to the top team on the results of strategic learning teams rather than store up the learning in a 'big-bang' approach.
5. Think well ahead about building pressures on the organization relative to capacity to sustain both learning and change into implementation.
6. Use the communication of outputs as a further opportunity for learning about how to implement change more effectively.
7. See strategic learning as a process of continual relevance and not as a one-off exercise.

LEARNING DON'TS

1. Don't compartmentalize the implementation process from the phases of analysis and choice.
2. Don't allow the facilitators to get so close to it that they assume that all the other key players are on the same point of the learning curve as they are.
3. Don't allow the MD or CEO to stand-off from the process at key phases so that it becomes difficult to re-immerse him or her in the thinking at a later stage.
4. Don't train middle managers to understand strategic issues and to implement change and then preclude them from full participation in the critical stages of implementation.
5. Don't exhaust managers in the analysis and choice phase to such a degree that they have little energy or enthusiasm to drive the change forward.
6. Don't spend too much time in trying to resolve specific agendas that are introduced without sufficient previous analysis and thought about options.
7. Don't involve managers in formulating a strategy and then delay and dilute the communication process.

Postscript

Following the strategic review, Dowty Communications continued a rapid programme of external refocusing and internal change. This was partly overtaken by external events as Dowty Group itself was taken over by TI Group. TI subsequently divested its telecommunications business to Cray where the original CASE business (as at 1993) is once again showing good profitability.

References

1. Grundy, A.N., *Implementing Strategic Change*, Kogan Page, 1993.
2. Johnson, E. and Scholes, K., *Exploring Corporate Strategy*, Prentice-Hall, 1988.

6
Steering implementation at Mercury Communications

6.1 Introduction and background

Mercury Communications is the subsidiary of the multinational company, Cable and Wireless. Mercury's operations are principally in the UK and Mercury has made major inroads to the UK telecommunications market mainly at the expense of the former 'monopoly-holder', British Telecommunications (or BT).

Mercury Communications has expanded extremely rapidly. The company was founded in 1981 and was awarded a licence in 1983, but its principal growth has occurred since 1985. By 1993 its turnover exceeded £1 billion. Its growth has mainly occurred through providing high quality telephony to large corporations initially centred on the City of London. It now has UK coverage and over the last few years has extended its activities into the long-distance residential telephone market. By 1993 Mercury was adding 20 000 new residential customers each month. (This is comparable to the rate of market penetration of the highly successful First Direct telephone banking in the UK. By coincidence, Mercury's managing director was previously MD at First Direct.)

In the late 1980s Mercury's pace of expansion was thus faster than that of Apple Computers, reflecting its success in penetrating the UK market. This rapid progress was facilitated by Mercury's flexible organization.

This case on steering implementation takes us right into the heart of Mercury Communications. At the time of the case Mercury was structured in a number of major business areas and within one of these (Mercury Data) we find a key business unit, Mercury Messaging. Mercury Messaging is a microcosm of what was happening in the wider Mercury organization.

Mercury Messaging was recently formed from two separate units – Telex and Electronic Messaging Groups – with somewhat differing cultures. Subsequent to this case, Mercury Messaging now comprises three groups, also including Facsimile Services. At the time of the case, Mercury Messaging boasted the highest turnover and contribution to profit per employee of any business unit within Mercury.

Traditionally, Mercury Messaging showed good growth and good profits. Staff energies were more focused on meeting business needs (mainly growth) than on, primarily, being profit-driven, cost conscious and continuously improving the business's competitive position. While a high premium was put on sustaining flexibility, which had been an important critical success factor, this needed to be balanced against the need for focus and disciplined process in the organization.

The senior team were already well advanced in devising a strategy for future development of the business. Here the need was one of helping to steer implementation, particularly by improving organizational capability, not in devising a strategy. The case is described as follows:

– Origins of the initiative
– Planning the learning process
– Making it happen
– Extracting the benefits
– Lessons from the Mercury case.

6.2 Origins of the initiative

The general manager of Mercury Messaging, John Mittens, was becoming concerned about his staff's ability to implement the strategy, which was likely to stretch their capabilities much more than in the past. Despite his efforts to weld together a coherent team at all levels, and a good deal of patience, many staff appeared to be focused mainly on striving to be more efficient rather than more effective.

Very few staff had had much formal management development – their training had been primarily of a sales or technical nature. Most worked long hours, some of which was spent in resolving tactical problems rather than trying to understand and rectify the underlying causes of these problems. This situation was despite a quality initiative that had been in progress throughout the organization for some time.

All these symptoms seemed to point to a skills gap in the organization, and there was a danger that this gap might widen when the organization tried to implement its strategy for further development. John Mittens and

Mercury Messaging's human resources manager, Russell Connor met to discuss how they might tackle this issue.

Through a very close acquaintance, Russell knew of a consultant who had done a lot of work in the same industry but in a non-competing company. The consultant (by chance, the author of this case) had been perceived to be relatively successful in helping managers develop their individual skills by working in groups on key business issues.

John Mittens agreed to invite me to meet him and Russell Connor at Mercury Messaging's modern, high-tech-looking offices on London's Great West Road. After quick introductions and coffee had arrived, John Mittens rapidly explained the problem:

> You see, we have a number of staff, particularly those whose backgrounds are mainly sales/technical who we try to coach and direct but due to their limited experience they are often unable to come to grips with the basics of good management. For instance, when we pursue market opportunity they hardly seem to pause for breath before they are in the middle of the project. The result is that we have too many projects, many of which don't really fit with what we are trying to achieve overall. And the good ones we do have become disrupted when someone gets pulled off to do something more urgent.
>
> We also find that people are not really that cost conscious. Our engineers often buy new equipment (much of this being smaller items) which turns out to be a response to a one-off need. They, like most young engineers, don't seem to think through the applications, what the benefit/cost analysis is. They just need to get it because someone has said we really must be able to service some highly specific need.
>
> Don't get me wrong. I am painting a picture of our worst problems. We have achieved an awful lot by creating an energetic environment and stretching people, but I am concerned about burn-out and achievement of our longer-term objectives. Many of our staff are still relatively young and are in danger of continuing like this unless they can somehow switch over to a different way of managing.

Russell Connor then amplified what John had said:

> I think, Tony, we have a problem similar in many ways to your other client in a similar growth industry. Our industry has grown so rapidly that in the 1980s rush we really haven't built the management skills to survive the new world of the 1990s. We are now not just competing with BT but many other new players, which amplifies the challenge considerably. Our staff may not appreciate the level of competitive challenge.

John Mittens agreed:

> Although our senior team has put a lot of work into the strategy I don't think at our middle and lower levels that staff really appreciate how competitive the

market is becoming and what this means for how we do things around here. And even though the recession is now biting and we really need to tighten our costs, there is still an attitude of going for business with relatively little concern for costs or return on investment.

I then described my experiences elsewhere and how it was very likely that the problem was composed of a number of elements. Certainly there were some clear skills gaps that would be relatively straightforward to address. However, there was the more fundamental issues of style of working and of management systems and process. In addition, there was a lack of awareness of the competitive environment and as an organization, of how to implement change. This was a key issue especially as the business strategy might have some change implications. Finally, staff's capability in project managing tasks needed to be improved, and although the company was relatively young it was difficult to work in cross-disciplinary teams.

I decided to make the following proposal. I said that it seemed to me that we might be able to hit a number of birds with perhaps one (or at most two) stones, and the best way forward was probably for John Mittens and Russell Connor to think about a business action learning programme. This would consist of three parts. First, it would not just involve individual learning but also team and organizational learning. As Mercury Messaging was not a very large organization it would be feasible to share much of the learning across and upwards. Second, it would involve action-working on live issues with a view, subsequently, to implementing appropriate changes. Third, it would be business-focused, so that it would not be just action learning for the individuals involved *but would also help John Mittens solve some of Mercury Messaging's most important business issues.*

Finally, it would be a modular programme: it would not simply be a course. A series of workshops, learning projects and presentations would be devised that would make it a much more powerful vehicle for learning and change.

6.3 Planning the learning process

In less than an hour we had sketched out the process and content of a learning programme that would deal with four key business issues identified by John Mittens.

The overall process is shown in Figure 6.1. Prior to the core workshop, further work was done to refine the 'key issues' into a series of four questions, one for each of the four learning projects.

The four issues that were chosen (see Figure 6.2) were as follows:

MANAGING FOR COMPETITIVE AND FINANCIAL
ADVANTAGE

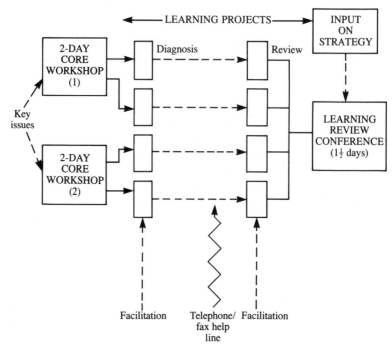

Figure 6.1   Strategic learning within Mercury Messaging: the process

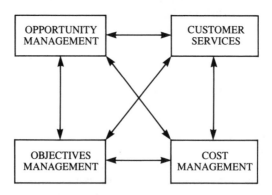

Figure 6.2   Mercury Messaging's four learning projects

1. *Opportunity management*: this project focused on how new opportunities were screened and evaluated.
2. *Objectives management*: this addressed how individual managers could link their personal goals with project and wider business objectives.
3. *Customer services*: this focused on how customer services could be managed for greater competitive (and financial) advantage.
4. *Cost management*: this aimed at exploring how costs could be managed much more effectively and in a way closely related to the business strategy.

Figure 6.2 shows the four projects networked together. Many of the issues arising in individual projects had implications for other learning projects.

Each of the four projects was defined by a key question, as follows:

LEARNING PROJECT 1: OPPORTUNITY MANAGEMENT

Mercury Messaging (MM) faces a large number and variety of opportunities for business development of variable attractiveness, not all of which it can or should respond to. How can MM improve its process for identifying, screening, evaluating, deciding on and finally programming:

– strategic opportunity?
– tactical opportunity?

What barriers to change would need to be surmounted to achieve this?

LEARNING PROJECT 2: OBJECTIVES MANAGEMENT

Mercury Messaging's external and internal environment is subject to rapid change. What should be the role of objectives (strategic, operational and financial) in steering a path through this change, and how can these objectives be used to greater effect in the business?

LEARNING PROJECT 3: COST MANAGEMENT

In an increasingly competitive market, which has now been aggravated by a recession, Mercury Messaging is about to make significant reductions in its expenses for budgetary purposes. How can this be done without damaging the business:

– short term?
– long term?

In what specific areas do you see possibilities for improving leverage between the use of resource and value added?

LEARNING PROJECT 4: PEOPLE MANAGEMENT

How Mercury Messaging recruits and develops, deploys and motivates its people may be an important variable in determining its competitive advantage. In what areas can the people management process be improved in order to generate further competitive and financial benefits at minimum cost and what barriers to change might need to be overcome?

Of these four learning projects, the core issue was that of opportunity management. This was an area with greatest potential impact on the business. It was also the area where *most change* was accomplished.

The core workshops

About a dozen managers attended each of the two core workshops, which were run on alternate weeks. The content of each two-day workshop, at which I facilitated full time, was as follows:

DAY 1

– Introduction, objectives, positioning.
– Case on competitive change: the car industry.
– What does this mean to us?
– What do we now need to do to compete?
– How do we evaluate new business opportunities?

DAY 2

– How competitive and financial advantage are linked.
– Financial awareness: managing costs and reaching break-even.
– Basic principles: project management.
– Introduction to the learning projects.
– What tools do we need for the job?: managing change frameworks.

The two-day workshop comprised an array of inputs and activities. However, by focusing an analysis of Mercury Messaging's business issues and by using just one case from elsewhere it proved possible to achieve this coverage without resulting in a superficial 'learning skim'. One factor of major assistance was the liveliness of programme participants. They seemed to learn at a rate similar to the speed with which they conducted their everyday jobs. I found that they were able to learn roughly half as quickly again as managers in slower-moving environments.

Following the core workshops each learning project team spent approximately half a week in sessions as a group to work on the project issue. In addition, they also spent some individual time in further analysis. The workshops extended over a two-and-a-half-month period, and in the interim, although not always in attendance, I facilitated via telephone/fax helpline, which was very actively used.

It was felt best to give the groups in each team between two and three months to work on their learning projects, as a shorter period would have not done justice to the issues and a longer period would probably have resulted in a loss of momentum.

Not only did the learning projects cover issues to do with managing change, project management and team working, but they also gave managers more opportunity to practise business analysis tools discussed in the core workshop. It was probably because of this that I felt comfortable about covering so much ground in the core workshop. In effect, the action-based nature of the programme allowed considerable learning synergies to be gained.

Each project had a project plan and an appointed project coordinator. The managers were also given on-line access to John Mittens as key stakeholder. In order to enhance learning on working in teams, all participants took a Belbin team role test. This proved very useful, not so much in stereotyping individuals as 'only a plant', 'only a shaper' or 'only a chairman', but individuals were encouraged to develop those team roles that did not come quite as naturally to them.

The project activities culminated in a project review workshop. Here, I provided input to test and reshape presentations, taking care not to over-facilitate and over-intrude on each team's ownership of outputs.

Finally, all four learning projects were presented at a review conference attended by all managers in a hotel at the top of Richmond Hill. This conference lasted an intensive one and a half days (beginning at 5 pm in the evening). The format for the presentations was:

– present the project outputs: 'What we found out'
– present 'What we learned about the process, tools, etc., and about wider organizational issues'
– debate and constructive critique
– facilitator's summary on the outputs *and on* the process.

In addition, John Mittens was able to spend time formulating a strategic overview that put the projects into a wider context.

At the end of this phase of strategic learning, the issue that crystallized in many of the participants' minds was:

> We have analysed these four problem areas and reached some choices. In other areas we are still not quite clear on the way forward. But overall, we need to forge some implementation plans. So how do we do it? Do we do it on our own? Do we invite Tony to continue to facilitate?

Mercury Messaging thus decided to extend the learning process into a second phase. The four learning projects were re-labelled as 'change projects'. After some adjustment in team membership, the four teams were then given the task of developing clear and detailed implementation plans.

6.4 Making it happen

A number of steps were taken to forge successful implementation plans. First, the forces that enabled or constrained achievement of each project's key change objective were identified, analysed and evaluated. A particularly useful technique invented by one group was to draw up a force-field diagram[1] which depicted:

– the forces enabling and constraining change *as they were perceived to be now*
– the forces that were necessary *as a minimum* to move the change forward.

This highlighted some very important gaps that could then be presented to John Mittens and the senior team openly and directly, without being seen as an exercise in axe-grinding.

Second, as the teams now had more specific objectives and targeted outputs than they had originally, they found it easier to adopt a learning routine. On the other hand, there were some signs, in one or two of the groups, of resistance to revisiting earlier concepts. The urge towards 'freeze thinking' became very strong indeed.

John Mittens played a key role in ensuring that the learning/change projects did not terminate prematurely just after the Richmond conference. It would have been very easy to have expected 'things simply to happen', but he maintained an active involvement in the initial stages of implementation. This was despite a six-week part-time secondment around that time elsewhere in Mercury Communications.

A number of *process* lessons emerged from the four projects:

1. During the diagnosis stage, the definition of the problem changed quite

considerably. In some cases, the scope of the problem (and thus the project) seemed to grow. Learning project teams need to understand that to a degree this is inevitable as they learn more about the issues and their underlying causes.

2. Teams devoted at least half a day per week to the projects together (in addition to further investigations carried out individually). This put an additional burden on their workload. Again, it is essential to set their expectations realistically for the level of input required for the projects. It may be useful to couple this with a renewed effort in task effectiveness and time management in their day-to-day responsibilities.

   Also, at times it was difficult to get the teams together as a quorum because of other business pressures. This highlights the need to give (and sustain) a sufficiently high level of priority for the projects *vis-à-vis* other activities.

3. It may be easy to detect major contrasts between the more *structured* work within the learning process and other concurrent management activities that may appear to be more haphazard. This contrast of style may begin to generate cynicism that management are serious in desiring this change. Management need to be aware of these perceived discrepancies and be prepared to address them positively rather than compartmentalize them. Staff, in turn, need to manage any tendencies towards cynicism and put themselves in the position of more senior management who may seek to change behaviour and management style, but quickly suffer relapse.

6.5   Extracting the benefits

The key benefits from the four learning and change projects are detailed below.

Opportunity management

Mercury Messaging created a more formal and thorough process for screening and evaluating new product/market/technology opportunity. This involved not merely looking at the financial and sales projections but also the inherent strategic attractiveness of the opportunity externally, and also Mercury Messaging's competitive position and to what extent this could be sustained.

A series of bullet-point questions was drawn up and tested against past opportunities (good and not-so-good) in order to pilot the appraisal device. One of the problems was the level of detailed analysis to be done at the initial screening phase versus that at the more in-depth evaluation process. After considerable debate it was elected to adopt a common framework for both better screening and detailed evaluation. This approach proved to be simple and workable. To give you a flavour of the headings, they were structured along the following lines:

1. Is the market that the opportunity addresses inherently attractive and thereby offering above-average profitability?
2. Do we have competitive advantage and can this be sustained?
3. Will the financial returns be sufficient?
4. Given our resources and capability, can we implement it effectively?

Mercury Messaging's managers succeeded in being remarkably open about lessons from past projects. This was facilitated by the declaration of an 'amnesty': that Mercury Messaging managers could be totally open about lessons from past projects without fear of retribution. Outputs from this area were equivalent to Zone C, 'Inspiration', in Figure 2.7.

Objectives management

Progress on this issue was slightly more difficult to achieve. The project team and senior management agreed that staff ought to have a clearer framework of individual and team objectives, linked to business objectives. They also agreed on the *content* of these objectives. What was more difficult, however, was resolving the issue of *flexibility*.

On the one hand, Mercury Messaging wanted to preserve as much flexibility of goals and objectives as possible; but, on the other, everyone realized that taken to an extreme this fluidity made it more difficult to achieve goals owing to ever-changing priorities. This feature is by no means unique to Mercury Messaging; to a lesser or greater extent all organizations face this dilemma. When a company is grappling with major external (and internal) change this dilemma can become acute.

Another factor that complicated dealing with this issue was the need to take into account appraisal processes. This was thus shared with several other business units, but it proved difficult to effect local changes to appraisal processes to make a workable framework of objectives.

The mixed progress on establishing a more refined framework of objectives reflected the problem of shifting 'how we do things around here' (and were in Zone C of Figure 2.7).

Cost management

Although the members of this team had a particularly difficult time at the early, diagnosis stage they went on to produce some very useful insights, and identified a number of areas for more effective cost management. The following lists some of the key outputs from the project:

1. A number of areas were identified where *cost monitoring systems* could be significantly improved.
2. A much more *cost-aware* culture was created where staff began to challenge, continuously, whether objectives could be achieved with less cost.
3. In one specific area, the potential for some *very major cost savings* was highlighted.

On the final point above, it was interesting how the insights finally crystallized. During the Richmond conference discussion of whether or not cost area X was or was not one where significant savings could be achieved was losing momentum. I handled this as follows:

> So what you are all saying is that area X is a fixed cost, it is an unavoidable cost; these costs are necessary to run the business; they are costs which you are committed to contractually.
>
> I accept that some areas of cost are fixed, and are fixed longer-term, but usually there is some latitude and choice. In all the other companies I have consulted with there have always been *some things you can do* to mitigate fixed costs like this ... [the conference remained silent]
>
> But I suppose I just don't understand the technology. I admit I am beaten, the dog has been barking up the wrong tree... but all the same, it is very peculiar....

After this subtle pretence, one of the group (at the back) in a fairly quiet voice began:

> I think Tony might have a point here. For instance, there are at least some of our commitments to X which we might usefully review....

This was rapidly reinforced by a number of other voices, in ascending volume, until the full picture of the potential for managing cost area X more effectively fully crystallized.

Subsequent to the Richmond conference, Mercury Messaging saved some considerable sums through implementing change in how cost X was managed (mixing Zone A, 'Vision', and Zone B, 'Blind Spot', in Figure 2.7).

Customer services

This project was a mixture of customer-focus issues, organization and cost issues. The project team had to ensure that they retained a clear focus throughout – as a result of this diversity of issues. Nevertheless, it proved possible to crystallize a number of options for refocusing and concentrating the resources of Mercury Messaging's customer services activities.

Coordinating the outputs across projects

As is now evident, there were a number of interlinked issues between projects. To some extent the teams managed to draw these out themselves, but further input was provided to enable all four teams to view the entire process. For instance, key linkages were evident:

- between opportunity management and cost management: more effective choice of those opportunities that would help significantly reduce costs;
- between objectives and cost management: a clearer framework of objectives would help make staff manage resources more effectively, and again, reduce cost;
- between cost management and customer service: the cost/benefit analysis of proposed options to refocus customer services was itself done via investment appraisal of tangible and less tangible benefits and costs, including the costs of change and disruption.

Looking back, the final process of steering implementation had three phases (see Figure 6.3): the learning process, the change process and routinization. As an additional output, John Mittens was able to refine his mission and

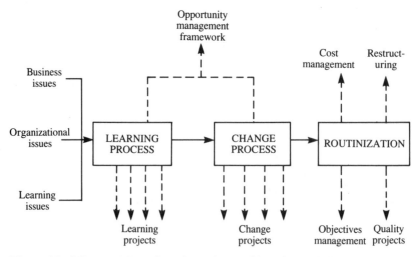

Figure 6.3 Mercury Messaging: three phases of learning and change

strategy statement for Mercury Messaging. This was essential to provide a focus point for the Richmond conference, and to provide direction to the objectives and opportunity management projects.

But the main output of the process was the opportunity management framework. This was fully incorporated into the organization's planning and control routines, helping it to sustain its past record of profitable growth. This was useful as it provided a more structured decision-making process, yet one that was consistent with the need to preserve flexibility.

6.6 Lessons from the Mercury case

The Mercury case yields lessons on applying strategic learning in three key areas:

– business outputs
– organizational outputs
– the learning process.

Business outputs

1. Strategic learning can be a powerful way of refocusing how an organization, such as Mercury Messaging, facing complex choices, deals with new business opportunity.
2. It can also generate some major cost savings without damaging competitive advantage. This demands concerted follow-through of the issues and attention to the major issues rather than the minutae.
3. It may be necessary to tailor notions of 'strategy' and 'mission' to a particular organizational context so that management do not operate with an inappropriate and rigid model. At Mercury Messaging management eventually realized that strategy needed to be formulated as a broad direction, supported by some specific targets. This was made workable by setting criteria for the type of opportunities in which they would be prepared to invest and in which they would not.

Organizational outputs

1. In a rapidly growing or changing organization you need some process, but not so much that it constrains. Although at Mercury Messaging the attempt to develop a framework for objectives did not appear to deliver its intended outputs, the real benefits were obtained through management realizing that a formal framework would not be workable.
2. One of the key benefits of strategic learning can be that of *team-building*.

In the Mercury case the managers got to know each other much better through the cross-functional project teams, and this proved to be an important benefit.

The learning process

1. Strategic learning programmes need the active and symbolic involvement of the top manager (as was the case at Mercury Messaging).
2. Sometimes the outputs from the learning process are unexpected. For instance, at Mercury Messaging a workable framework of objectives did not materialize, but managers learned to work more closely with one another. This resulting improvement in communication did a great deal to resolve 'the problem'. Partly as a result of the programme, Mercury Messaging developed a single culture. It is often easy to overlook softer benefits like this in retrospective appraisal of an intervention.
3. The benefits of strategic learning can often lag the initial intervention. Some of the benefits are surface-level (the initial learning) but others reflect deeper shifts in underlying perspectives. These shifts may become active subsequently only after a lull (which is often associated with initial implementation difficulties and a resulting energy-dip). This can be represented pictorially as in Figure 6.4, where the amplifying effect of other projects or initiatives (as occurred at Mercury Messaging) can be felt.

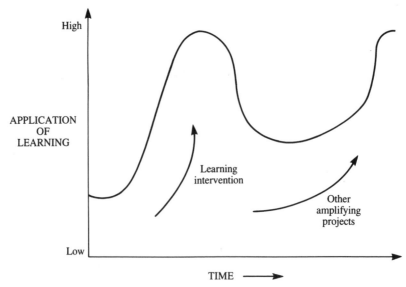

Figure 6.4 Assessing the impact of strategic learning over time

4. A natural phenomenon is this energy-dip which stems from the 'can I now go back to my main job?' syndrome. Strategic learning can make intensive demands on managers' energies. Energy levels should not become over-depleted when the learning is used to drive the implementation over a prolonged period of time.
5. The value of strategic learning is hard to assess because much of the value is generated through intermingling with other initiatives (as shown in Figure 6.4). Learning interventions in particular may not add value that is sustainable until the process merges or even loses its separate identity (as at Mercury Messaging) within the organization. This makes it difficult to measure, with any precision, the value that has been added.

Menu of opportunities

Let us now look at our menu of opportunities for strategic learning. This, once again, highlights the very tangible benefits of strategic learning and also reinforces previous lessons on orchestrating the learning process in a particularly testing environment.

1. Strategic learning should be very clearly targeted.
2. These targets can embrace learning, specific change and shifts in organizational style.
3. Strategic learning needs to be well positioned and consistently supported by top management.
4. Strategic learning requires skilful facilitation.

Postscript

In addition to having a greater market share than all UK competitors combined, Mercury Messaging is now (in 1993):

- the largest electronic messaging company in Europe
- believed to be the most profitable in the world
- the largest international telex carrier in the world and is still growing at a time when the telex market generally has been declining by 20–30 per cent per annum
- a global company with sales channels on every continent.

John Mittens reflects on this that:

> The learning and change process did cause some real changes in attitudes and thinking in Mercury Messaging. Staff appreciated more that we (management) didn't always have all the answers.

Not only this but we really appreciated that staff could play an absolutely invaluable role in helping us manage the business more effectively.

For example, this year we had a new messaging product which was thrust upon us. This was a real 'dog' product. So we set up a special team of staff to 'save the product'. Not only did we relaunch this product successfully, based upon their ideas, but we did so without any special advertising or sales support.

The result surpassed our wildest hopes – this product is now so successful that we have been inundated with orders. The financial benefits are considerable, and that is an understatement. . . .

Going back, I am not sure that we would have trusted staff with such a strategic project before we had realized the potential of the learning and change projects.

John Mittens' final comment in 1993 is that:

We now have an outstanding track record built upon a new flat organization. This organization follows an interlocking strategy that requires mutual support from each department and product group.

References

1. Grundy, A.N., *Implementing Strategic Change*, Kogan Page, 1993.

PART THREE
A MENU OF STRATEGIC LEARNING

7
Scenario development at Shell

7.1 What types of scenario exist?

This chapter is the first, specific application of strategic learning that we shall look at in Part Three. It focuses on scenario development, which is a way of enriching managers' strategic vision and challenging their mental models of business and their place in it.

The chapter is based on Shell's experience of scenario planning. Shell's use of scenario planning is often associated with planning at the Group level and also with global scenarios. This association with Group strategy may obscure the potential for using scenarios for more specific applications. These may include, for example:

- country or regional scenarios
- industry-specific scenarios
- scenarios for emerging markets, or markets subject to unpredictable change
- scenarios specific to a strategic decision, or major project
- scenarios for organizational change.

At Shell, these more specific scenarios are called 'focused scenarios', and are pictorially represented in Figure 7.1, which displays the *possible* linkages between different kinds of scenarios. This figure does not represent the *actual* scenario linkages, as it may not be felt appropriate or worth while to complete the entire chain of scenarios. The figure does, however, highlight certain features:

1. The global scenario provides a feed-in to other, focused scenarios. This explains the importance attached by Shell to scenario-building at this level.
2. The global scenario feeds-in assumptions to individual country or regional scenarios. It may also provide further input to industry or

Figure 7.1 A system of scenarios

market-specific scenarios, and indeed to decision-specific scenarios. Finally, it may (through examining social and technology trends) be able to shape future views of both the longer-term organizational shape and style.

3. In addition, focused scenarios may provide inputs (as shown in the dotted lines at the periphery of Figure 7.1). An area of particular note is the feed-in of decision-specific scenarios and country scenarios to views of possible organizational change.

Future organizational shape is often particularly hard to envisage, so it may be fruitful to combine views of the future to establish their likely impact on the organization. Organizational scenarios are potentially a most useful application of scenario development, yet they are often the most underutilized.

In the main part of this chapter we demystify the idea of scenarios as learning vehicles by exploring:

– What senarios mean within Shell
– Scenarios as a learning process
– Wider implications of scenario development.

7.2 What scenarios mean within Shell

The view of a scenario within Shell is that it is: 'An internally consistent account of how the business environment might develop over time.'[1]

A scenario is thus an *account* of the future. It is arrived at by story-telling which depicts a possible future, and also the path from the present, which makes this future plausible. It is also *internally consistent*. This means that it makes sense in that the variables that go to make up the picture do not clash with one another, and the way in which they interact makes intuitive sense.

For Shell, a scenario is not a subjective account of the future; it is constructed by interactive debate and through group learning. For Shell: 'Scenarios must be plausible to a "critical mass" of managers in the Group.'[1]

It may be helpful to contrast scenarios with forecasts and projections. While forecasts and projections typically involve extrapolating existing trends (often translated into numeric variables), scenarios are essentially mental constructs. These constructs are primarily of a qualitative nature. They indicate 'what the world might be like', conjuring up a picture or a series of pictures of the future. They tap into managers' imaginations, yet they differ from pure fantasy in that they represent structured, informed and shared imagination.

Unfortunately, in many organizations the concept 'scenario' has become associated very closely with the use of a complex set of forecasts. Sometimes these forecasts or so-called 'scenarios' are almost purely financial. In its worst form, a sensitivity analysis is called a 'scenario', which is yet another example of a strategic term that has become popularized, being used for quite a different purpose than was originally intended.

Shell's view is not that the success or failure of a particular scenario is whether or not it actually happens; rather, the value of a scenario lies in:

– the way in which it opens up and extends managers' thinking about the future business environment, shifting their views of what might happen;
– testing particular strategies or decisions against various scenarios in order to test their robustness and flexibility; scenarios are seen as helping managers to 'think the unthinkable';
– providing a more informed means of scanning environmental change so that key changes can be identified, understood and acted upon much earlier; which helps to diminish the lag that occurs between sensing an issue, problem recognition, sharing and analysing the problem, and then evaluating options and commencing implementation.

Scenario development is thus a particularly interesting and challenging form of strategic learning. Indeed, planners within Shell were early proponents of the notion of 'Planning as learning'.[2]

7.3   Scenarios as a learning process

The four core elements of scenario planning in Shell are represented in Figure 7.2. This shows strategic vision as being crucial in driving views of Shell's competitive positioning and also of its strategic options. Both competitive positioning and option management are in close dialectic with one another.

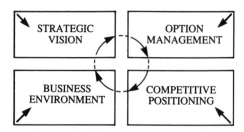

Figure 7.2   Ingredients of scenario development at Shell (produced with kind permission from Graham Galer, Shell International)

But where does the 'strategic vision' actually come from? As a process, it comes from managers and planners working in close concert with each other. From almost the beginning of scenario planning, Shell's planners sought to avoid the 'think tank' notion of the planners being experts on the world. Although their corporate planning is supported by economists and other specialists, this service division sees its main role as being one of facilitating strategic learning, rather than 'owning scenarios'.

In the last five years or so, the role of managers as strategic thinkers, and planners as learning facilitators, has been further strengthened. One of the key changes during this period is the increased use of strategic workshops to involve managers more centrally within scenario development. Graham Galer, whose interview is contained at length later in the chapter, describes how this works in practice.

Scenario planning in Shell has now become very much a 'way of life' both within its operating companies in live planning exercises, and also in off-line activities such as management development and training. Graham Galer tells us that:

> Things have changed considerably. Nowadays you only have to go into a management development course to find scenarios being developed as a learning process. These are often remarkably similar to those being developed elsewhere. Increasingly, the sense of any difference between planning and learning is becoming blurred.

Returning to the ingredients of scenario planning, the strategic vision depicted in Figure 7.2 requires further amplification. The building blocks of strategic vision are shown in Figure 7.3, which highlights some important points.

1. Scenario development requires an understanding of the key sources of instability – at a global, industry and possibly more micro level.
2. The reasons for discontinuity need to be thought through in depth.
3. In addition, more detailed analysis of the key variables that might impact on, or shape, the scenario is required.
4. This requires surfacing and examining the underlying driving forces that underpin these variables, and also examining the key interdependences between variables.
5. Finally, in order to explore how a possible scenario might occur, the dynamics of change may need to be understood in greater depth. Also, it

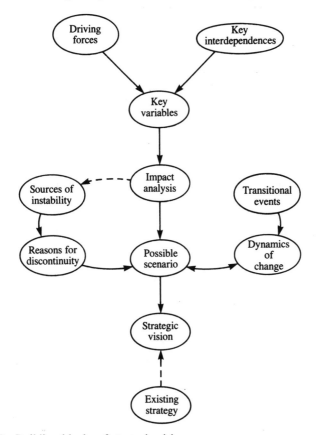

Figure 7.3   Building blocks of strategic vision

is important to think about the kind of transitional events that might be instrumental in bringing about this particular scenario.

To amplify the final point, transitional events can play a key role in assessing the plausibility of a given scenario. Scenarios need to be judged on a number of issues, including:

- their internal consistency
- the degree of challenge posed to managers' thinking (except for a 'stable' scenario)
- whether a train of transitional events, which might lead on to the scenario, can be assembled that could quite *easily occur* (but does not mean that they will *probably occur*).

It may be possible, for instance, to transpose similar events that are occurring elsewhere in the world, or have occurred in the past, onto the path of scenario development. This is relatively easy to do, for instance, with key political turning points. Other transitional events might include, for instance:

- a breakthrough in a new technology which reshapes the industry
- a new market area that has been a conceptual possibility becomes commercially viable, perhaps because a key player opens it up, or because of regulatory or other changes
- the onset of a recession or recovery
- a major disaster, natural or man-made.

The concept of a chain of transitional events bears some resemblance to that of 'alignment',[3] where a change in the environment crystallizes only when a number of key variables line up. If they don't line up, then a particular state of the world, that might have happened, refuses to crystallize.

Scenario development thus draws from 'systems thinking'[4] – seeing the business environment and the business itself as a complex series of overlapping systems. This explains why interdependences between variables are so important to analyse, and also why, when doing impact analysis, it is so important to consider the 'cross impact' of variables. This helps managers explore what might happen if one particularly important but uncertain variable impacts on another, similar, one. Note the dotted line between impact analysis and sources of instability in Figure 7.3.

As you may have detected by now, scenario planning is not for those who seek simple, simplistic answers to complex issues. Even Figure 7.3 may look sophisticated, but it belies the fact that these activities may need to iterate not just once, but possibly a number of times.

Scenario development is, however, a learning process in which there is a learning curve. The first run for a management team may prove very taxing (but equally rewarding – in a green-field site), but subsequent attempts will prove a lot easier.

At this juncture, it is perhaps best to learn more about scenario planning from a manager at Shell. Graham Galer, of Shell Group Planning, explains how it feels to use scenario planning and illustrates what this methodology can achieve.

ORIGINS OF SCENARIO PLANNING

I suppose it all began in the late 1970s. Scenario planning in Shell started out as a response to the increasingly turbulent environment with oil shocks, political disturbances and economic volatility. But most of our earlier work in scenario planning was done in response to ad hoc requests.

It was only really in 1981 that the methodology was made more coherent. At that time a major review of Shell's planning systems was undertaken. This, in effect, institutionalized scenario planning. It is now very much part of our approach to management of the business.

Where scenario planning fits in

You can't go for long within Shell before you hear the word 'scenario'. It would be a rare speech from a senior manager that did not mention the word. Indeed, we are often asked to draft substantial parts of these addresses, covering top management's view of scenarios. This is very interesting – in the very act of delivering the speech, the speaker may have reinforced existing ideas or even internalized new ideas into his thinking.

Planning in Shell splits into two major types, although obviously they interrelate closely. The principal use of scenario thinking is in strategic planning. This is very much our concern at Group, but as Shell consists of relatively autonomous operating companies (or 'Opcos') there is obviously a good deal of strategic thinking at a company level, too.

We tend to regard this as a separate activity from business planning which is more concerned with allocating resources needed to implement agreed strategies. Typically this is a lot more numerically based.

Broadly speaking, we do a major review of our global scenarios every two or three years. We put a great deal of work into these scenarios, but these by no means account for all our work as there is a lot more to it, as I will explain.

The potential and pitfalls of scenarios

I shall now come back to the reasons for scenarios, and the problems we experience with planning.

Scenario planning differs greatly from what went before – this has already been well documented, so I shan't cover old ground again. Basically, we wanted to move forward from single views of the future environment and this meant we needed to explore uncertainty in much greater depth.

When we started developing scenarios we faced a number of problems. First, when it began we tended to carry out a study, go away and come back with the result, then try to involve management later on. This gave rise to obvious problems of ownership which we have taken great pains over many years to avoid.

We try to minimize the risk of groupthink by conducting interviews with a wide range of managers internally. We also supplement this with external interviews outside Shell.

A second problem that we always have to avoid is ... groupthink. There is always a danger of falling into this trap but I think our track record on scenarios of avoiding problems like this is pretty good.

Focused scenarios – developing scenarios – beginning the process

I shall now describe how we might set about a typical scenario project. Perhaps it is best to focus on some of the more recent, specific work we have done. We tend to call these 'focused scenarios' as they deal with more localized or specific issues than the broader, global scenarios.

We often get requests to do ad hoc work in various parts of the world. This now forms a good proportion of our work. First of all, we try to get started by doing a bare skeleton – if you like a quick and dirty version of a scenario.

Imagine that we are in one of Shell's Opcos. As I stressed, we involve local management very much in the process. So we might begin by getting the managers to think individually about the factors in the business environment that are important. We would then take a look at the existing trends in order to explore the continuities and possibly any gradually emerging discontinuities.

The other angle we focus on is those factors which appear to be particularly uncertain.

What we then do is build up the scenario around the *key uncertainties* which I shall say more about later. We would follow the work by managers individually pooling their ideas. In fact, over recent years we have very much relied upon workshops to provide some structure and a learning environment to support scenario development.

This whole theory of importance and uncertainty is simple but is of some significance. What we are then able to do is to get managers to think about the relative degree of importance (and also the degree of uncertainty) of all of the key factors. This helps isolate the factors with greatest potential impact in shaping a different world to that prevailing at present.

To support the process we use devices such as post-it notes in the form of magnetic, hexagonal shapes. We then write the appropriate factor on each shape and position each one on a magnetic board. This allows managers to play with what they see as the relative importance and relative uncertainty for different issues. This is achieved by shifting the shapes relative to one another. After a while managers are then happy that they have prioritized the factors appropriately.

We might also, at that point, draw in the axis of a matrix in four quadrants to frame the factors that are of particular interest. But the really important bit is the moving around of the factors relative to each other.

You may note that this is a highly *qualitative* process. Scenario-building is very much about qualitative analysis. And that is why it is such a rich learning medium. It frees up managers' minds to explore the issues in new ways.

Its particular strength is to get the right things on to the management agenda. What matters really is very much the quality of debate that comes through. This is of equal, if not more, importance than the final output.

Developing the scenarios: building up

So far I have described how we break down the future environment. But we also need to build up in order to create a scenario. Based on the earlier analysis of key factors we would then explore the underlying driving forces in greater depth. This would be done with particular focus on those factors considered most important, and most uncertain.

We would then try to develop story lines for how a future might be shaped and what it would then look like. Besides the driving forces we would be particularly interested in any special events that might tend to lead the world to develop in a new and different way. With localized scenarios we would focus on the kind of local events that could happen. This is a particularly fruitful area for local managers to input to. These local events may kick start a particular scenario.

It is also helpful to then look at the dynamic paths that might lead from the present to the future state of the world described in the scenario. This is quite a creative point as you need to imagine what events (and knock-on events) might occur – and what they might do to the overall scenario.

Global scenarios

With our global scenarios we obviously have to consider an array of events. The interesting thing here is to consider combinations of events. To help with this we sometimes write key events on cards and then look at particularly interesting dynamic sequences.

The number of scenarios we might look into depends very much on the context. No, we don't necessarily look at just two – or three for that matter – although we usually end up with a maximum of three, for management convenience.

Building scenarios: facilitation

I mentioned earlier the importance of the quality of debate. This depends a good deal on the quality of facilitation. We spend a lot of time training people before they begin live facilitation – it isn't something that you can just do because of your expert knowledge – far from it.

What we particularly try to avoid is the facilitator style that is very mechanical – one that just gets people through the workshop. It isn't just a set of tasks. We all have slightly different styles but these still work within the same basic methodology.

I think it might help to examine a recent case of scenario building so that you can get a better feel for how it actually works.

This example involved a fast developing country where there are some major political uncertainties, which I think I shall call ... Bravda.

An example: scenarios for Bravda

I got a call from the general manager in Bravda. He wanted to run a scenario check in more depth over this country's strategy. We have been involved in Bravda for quite a long time as a Group – we are also pretty big there. There is also a history of scenario planning there which goes back many years.

There are some major changes looming in the country and we also have some interesting opportunities there. Looking back this stands out as an ideal application for scenarios. But the real trigger for this exercise was that a sufficient number of people felt that they 'didn't understand the situation terribly well'. Not only has the environment changed a lot in Bravda but we were dealing with totally new people – not only within management but also in terms of the planning staff involved, too.

We first agreed exactly what we would do with the local general manager. We also agreed the need for us, as planners, to be involved in checking out the scenarios by comparison with our existing Group scenarios.

The exercise was very interesting as the resulting Bravda scenarios were rather different from one another in their views of how the environment might unfold. But of particular interest is the scenario-making *process* rather than just the content. This exercise was especially challenging as there was always the danger of doing undue damage to local morale by pushing one of the more extreme scenarios quite far.

But we were successful in getting a balance between challenge and support. You asked me particularly about the role of the learning process, particularly in relation to possible denial of possibilities because of build-up of commitment. The Bravda example was clearly one where we *might* have been in some danger on this score. However, the general manager, who was widely travelled within the Group and a long-standing Shell man, achieved an admirable balancing act.

He managed to wear two hats – one in leading the local team and the other in reflecting his Group conscience – he also needed to take the broader view.

The Bravda scenarios lead me on to another point. One of the key uncertainties is always the timing of particular key events. We usually deal with this by looking at how these key events would impact on our short- and longer-term development plans, but we don't try to refine it much more than that. I really think that it is a bit too stretching to ask managers to make more specific predictions than this about when these key events might occur. We are not looking for the impossible in scenario planning; although I accept that sometimes the impact of key events might be aggravated by their particularly unfortunate timing.

If I may, I shall begin to summarize, as a meeting for our next project is due to start in about ten minutes' time. Scenario planning is very much an art, and not a science. It is a creative and qualitative exercise in analysis – it isn't business modelling in the conventional sense. It is mental modelling, but you really couldn't map the mental processes at work, they are just too complex to do that. Also, we gain expert input from our economists, who highlight some important things.

Its application varies within Shell depending upon the degree of local enthusiasm and also the particular context – in business, geographic and historical terms. For instance, in one major country they were so enthusiastic about using scenario workshops that our original series of events with them was subsequently cascaded down to some quite deep levels in the organization.

While we do facilitate focused scenarios we do find more difficulty in encouraging managers to work up scenarios for major strategic decisions or projects. That said, there is already a lot of strategic data readily available to feed into these decisions. And also, if the decision involves an extension from our existing strategy then this may trigger an ad hoc exercise.

But I can understand the reluctance of the champion who has had to put an awful lot of energy in to make a project happen not to want it tested vigorously against scenarios. We already have enough hurdles without posing more. But, on the other hand, there is the argument that the project should be tested against scenarios to get a better idea of the risks we are undertaking. There has been quite a lot of discussion on this issue.

Overall, I think we have succeeded in creating the circumstances in which the individual can learn through the scenario process. But this goes hand in hand with the prior knowledge of that individual that the learning can be taken on board by the company.

We provide adequate resources to encourage scenario development. We also strive hard to pull scenario thinking into key decisions. Scenario planning is a key part of our corporate glue. I mentioned previously that Shell is relatively decentralized – scenarios are a major vehicle for the centre to add value. Indeed, they have become a part of our corporate culture.

7.4 Wider implications of scenario development

The Shell case highlights a number of wider implications for the use of scenarios in other organizations, as follows:

1. *Positioning*: in Shell scenarios are positioned very centrally in the organization. This has enabled the process to be taken very seriously and has helped it become an important part of the Shell culture. The extent of senior involvement in the process has helped spread a *learning culture* within Shell. In some ways the idea of a learning culture may be more helpful than that of 'the learning organization'. In Shell's case, for instance (and this is most likely to be mirrored in larger diverse

organizations), the idea of a 'learning organization' is probably too large and abstract as a single concept without the following embellishment. In addition to the learning culture, learning is facilitated by learning process skills, and also a learning strategy which helps direct the learning. Figure 7.4 thus depicts strategic learning as a number of key, mutually supporting elements.

2. *Disseminating learning*: scenarios are a very powerful vehicle for disseminating strategic learning throughout the organization. This may help alleviate some of the hurdles of linking strategy to implementation that were explored at great length in Chapters 5 and 6.

3. *Facilitation*: the Shell case underlines the importance of developing facilitation capability. This is not a skill that all people are born with – some individuals are better at it than others, as they are more able to hold personal judgement in suspense and are more able to manage process than others. It also demands considerable practice to have these skills.

4. *Ownership*: as we found in previous chapters, ownership is a key issue. This becomes an even greater issue the more complex the learning process, and thus the greater the need for facilitation. Where the facilitators have their own power base (as in the Shell experience), and there are additional issues of local versus Group loyalties, clarity of 'who owns what' is absolutely critical.

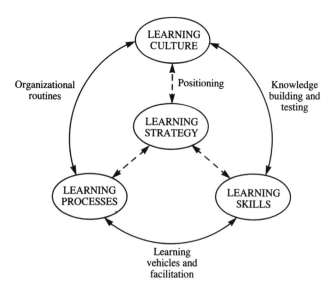

Figure 7.4 Strategic learning and the learning organization

5. *Commitment*: the Shell case highlights, once again, the tension between strategic learning and strategic commitment. Management may have greater commitment to a strategy than may be justified by their cumulative learning. This is a factor highlighted by Ghemawat[5] where, in some instances of rapid build-up of commitment, commitment itself burns up faster than the rate of learning. Scenarios offer one way of accelerating learning as they not merely surface existing strategic assumptions, but they also generate additional ones. These also probe deeply into zones of greatest importance and uncertainty.

6. *Strategic decisions*: at Shell, scenarios are used primarily to analyse global and country-level uncertainty and discontinuity. Their use for specific decisions (which one might call 'highly focused scenarios') is more limited. In the Shell environment most strategic decisions are well covered within the existing frame of scenarios. These scenarios are detailed and Shell also has in place clear notions of its competitive positioning and strategic options (see Figure 7.2). This makes highly focused scenarios less of an issue than elsewhere, except where there is a particularly large or risky project at stake, especially one that is outside Shell's core zone of strategic knowledge. The moral is that in other organizations there may well be equal or possibly more value to be gained out of highly focused scenarios dealing with specific, strategic decisions.

7. *Importance/uncertainty*: on a wider note, Shell's use of importance/uncertainty highlights the ability of this form of analysis to evaluate the assumptions underlying any strategic learning exercise. This tool can be used just as effectively for a small-scale project – or perhaps to understand key vulnerabilities in a new job role – as it can for a large-scale scenario development (see Figure 7.5).

Scenario development has thus provoked some additional insights on our analysis of strategic learning. These insights show, I believe, that scenario development has an important role to play, not only at the global or macro level but also at the micro level. We now continue our analysis by looking next at organizational capability and performance.

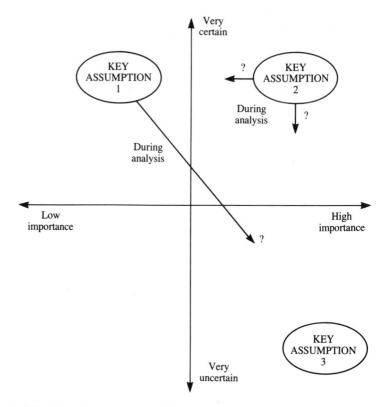

Figure 7.5 Mapping importance and uncertainty – key assumptions. (Note: Variants of this matrix were proposed by Mitroff, I.R. and Emshoff, J.R., 'On strategic assumption making: a dialectical approach to policy and planning', *Academy of Management Review*, vol. 4, no. 1, pp. 1–12 (1979) and are in use at Shell and elsewhere.

References

1. Galer, G. and Van Der Heijden, K., 'How planners create organisational learning', *Group Planning*, Shell International, 1973.
2. De Geus, A., 'Planning as learning', *Harvard Business Review*, March–April 1988, pp. 70–4.
3. Grundy, A. N., *Corporate Strategy and Financial Decisions*, Kogan Page, 1992.
4. Senge, P., *The Fifth Discipline: The Art and Practice of the Learning Organisation*, Century Business, 1990.
5. Ghemawat, P., *Commitment, the Dynamic of Strategy*, Macmillan, New York, 1991.

8
Organizational capability and performance

8.1 Managing in the round

In Part Two of this book, and in Chapter 7, we examined three cases –
Dowty, Mercury and Shell – to explore different phases of organizational
activity to which strategic learning can be applied.

Following the Shell case we now examine a different aspect of the issues.
In this chapter we discuss organizational capability and the way in which it
can be reshaped to improve performance. This is done by looking at a short,
composite case called 'Interspace', drawn from my diverse experiences of
companies trying to make major shifts in their capability.

Many organizations are reluctant to publicize their stories of changing
'how we do things around here' as a learning process, principally because
they feel they might expose themselves to error and cynicism. This highlights
not merely the sensitivity of this kind of learning process, but also that
claims to have made major breakthroughs in organizational behaviour
should be subjected to some skilful questioning rather than taken at face
value.

Let us now turn to the case.

8.2 Organizational change and learning at Interspace

Introduction

Over the past five years, Interspace Corporation has been undergoing a
major process of organizational change and learning geared to improving
business performance. In this case we see culture change, business and
management process redesign playing an integral role in making change
happen, and as a continual learning process.

The case runs as follows:

- Background and strategy to change at Interspace
- Business and management process redesign
- Lessons from the case.

Background and strategy to change at Interspace

In the late 1980s a major strategic change was about to reshape a major company operating in a service and technology intensive industry.

To meet the challenge of the 1990s, the top management of Interspace attempted to reshape and transform their existing culture. Management's vision was to build a 'world-class corporate culture' to respond to what was seen to be a much tougher international environment. This culture change was seen as being integral with strategy development and operational change, but how these all fitted together emerged only gradually as an organizational learning process.

After an initial period of diagnosis, by early 1990 the seeds for a more focused initiative to culture change had been sown. Top management had taken stock of Interspace's external and internal position and capability with selected help from external consultants. These were picked from a number of sources, from Europe, the US and from the Pacific Rim. The outputs from these various studies were several-fold. First, there were a number of outputs on Interspace's business strategies. Second, a major and comprehensive review of operational processes and practices was launched. This had a clear remit to 'simplify the business' wherever possible and thereby improve existing cost structures and flexibility. This initiative was known as 'IS': 'I' for international and 'S' for simplification.

Third, organizational structures progressed through a series of major changes which resulted in a flattening of past hierarchy, with more emphasis than ever before on business performance improvement.

This performance focus encouraged staff to direct their energies towards adding rather than destroying business value, and required a genuinely customer-driven orientation.

The change strategy was therefore targeted to improve Interspace's capability and performance by a combination of (a) external repositioning in the marketplace, (b) improvement in internal responsiveness (and thus added value to customers) by simplification and product improvement through innovation, and (c) reduction in costs. From the start, the culture change programme provided the framework through which management would continually challenge the status quo and learn how to run the business more effectively.

The early thrust of the change programme took the form of a series of workshops for managers at a variety of levels. The project manager of the 'IS' programme tells us that:

> At the beginning we just sat down and wondered where to start. In many ways we had to 'start from scratch' and try out a few approaches which we thought might work – for instance, through learning workshops with a behavioural impact.
> For instance, one of our approaches involved examining paradigm shifts. By getting people to identify 'how we do things around here' we found that it wasn't too difficult to get a pretty clear picture of our own paradigm. During one session we asked some of those managers who had been with us a long time to go out and burn 'the old' paradigm flip charts. They actually went outside and created a small bonfire with their 'old paradigm' flip charts. They were all smiling when they came back in.
> We found paradigms to be one of the *least* threatening areas of the change and learning processes. Ultimately it is up to you whether you shift your behaviours – a paradigm actually exists inside you – so you can choose; you can control your way of acting.

The Interspace Group employed over 30 000 world wide. This meant that change and organizational learning absorbed the efforts of more than 100 people (part time) acting as facilitators. The learning task was thus greatly amplified by the international spread of operations.

The 'IS' workshop programme then had a global initiation, which was coordinated by a central team. The initiation required extensive logistical planning and a dedicated co-ordinator freed from normal 'line' duties. Many of the facilitators were drawn from internal volunteers. This is a key point, as culture change initiatives elsewhere have been visibly undermined by managers who were volunteered by others 'as facilitators' and had inappropriate skills and style for this difficult role.

The approach to breakthrough management and continuous improvement taken was that of the Japanese philosophy of HOSHIN, which segregates large, quantum changes in the business ('breakthrough') from smaller, more incremental steps. HOSHIN also encourages *rotation* of initiatives so that each key organizational process is, in turn, scrutinized for improvement.

Business and management process redesign

As a key part of the process of continual improvement, a major programme of business and management process redesign was embarked upon to emphasize a business process-led structure. A strength of this programme was that, unlike many business process re-engineering (BPR) initiatives elsewhere, it did not neglect management processes such as strategic decision-making, people development and management controls. Management processes often escape unscathed because they are seen as potentially generating too much embarrassment if thoroughly scrutinized. Interspace is thus a relatively rare example of 'management process redesign', or what some call MPR.

Lessons from the case

The key lessons from the Interspace case are:

1. The process of culture change, and organizational change generally, is very much one of learning, and of iteration and refinement rather than necessarily getting it right first time.
2. Learning plays a core role in translating new and more open values into behaviour.
3. Major change typically goes through a number of stages. The pattern of these stages is sometimes only evident with hindsight, and managers need to search for and create these patterns through strategic learning.
4. Paradigm-breaking and challenging is a powerful vehicle for learning. (This is an important message to those UK companies or managers who are often afraid to grapple with paradigms.)
5. Change on this scale is often successful *because of* organizational interventions being conducted on a number of different but related fronts. The effect of this is to amplify organizational learning.
6. Strategic learning aimed at achieving major breakthroughs is supported by learning of a more tactical nature (for instance, through efforts for continuous improvement). Both forms of learning are not mutually exclusive: they overlap and are supportive of one another.
7. The HOSHIN approach of dividing breakthrough programmes from continuous improvement helps managers to deploy appropriate resources to learn about problems of different orders.

Before we conclude the Interspace case, I would like to highlight a major dilemma for programmes of major organizational change and performance improvement. Unless change is measured, how can those changes that are *sustainable* and *permanent* be distinguished from those that are only of temporary benefit? Yet this form of learning is difficult, and possibly tedious to the change catalyst. It may actually be intrusive. But a key learning lesson is that some way needs to be found to identify and track a few key (and as simple as possible) indicators of behaviour and performance shifts. To meet this need, a relatively small number of key indicators should be tracked, dealing with both 'hard' and 'soft' change.

8.3   Analysing capability and performance in your organization

Following the Interspace example, the second part of this chapter invites you to apply the framework in Figure 8.1 to your own business. If you would like to practise this first as a case simulation, then please read Appendix I (the AZP case) before resuming Chapter 8 at this point.

The utility of Figure 8.1 resides not in the parts of the analysis but in how it can be used to explore interrelationships. Capability and the performance that flows from capability come from *the whole* organizational system rather than from individual parts.

Analysing your own organization's capability

The following exercise is aimed at getting you to explore how the different pieces of the strategic jigsaw puzzle fit together in your organization to bring about capability. You should allow about 20 minutes (minimum) for this exercise. Each section focuses on one key element of the jigsaw puzzle and its interrelationships to the other elements. We deal in turn with:

– Quality
– Costs
– Skills

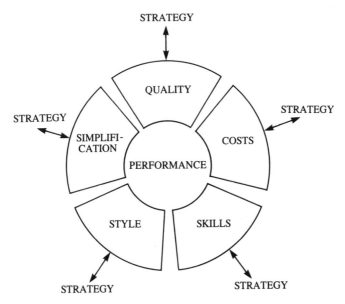

Figure 8.1   The strategic jigsaw puzzle

- Style
- Simplification
- Strategy.

Each element is related to each other in two ways. You will observe that each link is therefore covered *twice*, but each time covering a different aspect. They therefore deal with different issues.

You may wish to do a quick score of how you see your own organization, either as 1, 2 or 3 for each question.

Quality

1. Are there significant cost disadvantages associated with poor or uneven quality in your organization?

   - Insignificant   (3)
   - Significant   (2)
   - A lot   (1)

2. To what extent is the process of skills development a quality issue in your organization, or is it ill-focused/piecemeal? (quality and skills)

   - High quality   (3)
   - Medium quality   (2)
   - Low quality   (1)

3. Where you have adopted a quality management approach, is this sufficiently powerful to challenge inappropriate management style? (quality and style)

   - High challenge   (3)
   - Medium challenge   (2)
   - Low challenge   (1)

4. Does your quality management approach recognize the need to drive towards simplification rather than just to achieve higher quality in how things are *currently* done? (quality and simplification)

   - Quality and simplification are integral   (3)
   - Quality and simplification are loosely connected   (2)
   - Quality and simplification are seen as isolated   (1)

5. Does the business strategy have direct links into how your organization chooses to compete on quality (whether this is via differentiation, cost leadership or focus)? (quality and strategy)

– Close and direct links (3)
– Loose links (2)
– No real links (1)

Costs

1. Does your organization seek to achieve strategic targets for quality at lowest cost? (cost and quality)

– Clear and specific strategic targets set (3)
– Low, vague targets set (2)
– No real targets (1)

2. Are cost levels too high because of the wrong skills mix in the organization, implying a switch to fewer but higher quality staff (or vice versa)? (costs and skills)

– Skills mix is well aligned (3)
– Some imbalance exists (2)
– Major imbalance in skills mix exists (1)

3. Are cost levels high because of continual waste of resources through unnecessary management politics and empire building? (costs and style)

– There is no real waste of resources due to style (3)
– There is some waste (2)
– There is a lot of waste (1)

4. Are you implementing changes to drive costs down to competitive targets through simplification of processes? (costs and simplification)

– A major programme is under way or has been implemented (3)
– Piece-meal efforts are being made (2)
– No real focus on this (1)

5. Is the cost base so high (and unavoidably high) that we need to consider withdrawal from some areas of business? (costs and strategy)

– No need to review; the strategy exists because of
  existing cost advantages (3)
– Some areas may need retuning (2)
– A major need exists to review business scope in some areas (1)

Skills

1. What skills do we have for managing costs for both competitive and

financial advantage (e.g. cost awareness) and do these need significant improvement? (skills and costs)

- Ample skills exist for managing costs and financial
  advantage   (3)
- Some skills exist, but these are patchy   (2)
- Few skills exist to do this effectively   (1)

2. Do managers have the required interpersonal skills and resulting self-confidence needed in order to manage more openly? (skills and style)

- Ample interpersonal skills exist   (3)
- Some skills gaps exist   (2)
- Lots of skills gaps exist   (1)

3. Do we have the skills necessary (for instance, interpersonal, project management, change management and cross-functional business awareness) to manage major simplification programmes? (skills and simplification)

- Ample skills   (3)
- Some skills gaps exist   (2)
- Lots of skills gaps exist   (1)

4. Do we have the skills to implement quality programmes across the organization ('hard' and 'soft' skills)? (skills and quality)

- Ample skills   (3)
- Some skills gaps exist   (2)
- Lots of skills gaps exist   (1)

5. Do we have the skills not just to think strategically but also to implement the strategy (and any necessary change) effectively? (skills and strategy)

- Ample skills   (3)
- Some skills gaps exist   (2)
- Lots of skills gaps exist   (1)

Style

1. Does our management style inhibit the development of skills – for example, for managing across functional projects or for participation in major strategic decisions by middle managers? (style and skills)

- Management style facilitates skills development at all levels   (3)
- Management style is sometimes constraining   (2)
- Management style is often a block   (1)

2. Does our management style represent a major constraint in simplifying the business because we seem to enjoy complexity for its own sake? (style and simplification)

- Management style facilitates skills development at all levels (3)
- Management style is sometimes constraining (2)
- Management style is often a block (1)

3. What style of quality management has been adopted and what are the likely effects on performance (for instance, a culture-pull style versus a regulatory-push style with BS 5750/ISO 9000)? (style and quality)

- Balance a focus of pull and push (3)
- Imbalanced in some areas (2)
- Quality management has become either a ritual or just another set of routines (1)

4. What are the effects of our management style on the process of cost management? (style and cost)

- Management style provides a very open debate on costs (3)
- Management style encourages limited debate on costs of uneven quality (2)
- Management style prevents open and quality debate on costs (1)

5. Is our management style one that is consistent with, or at loggerheads with, achievement of the business or corporate strategy? (style and strategy)

- Total consistency (3)
- Mostly consistent, but some inconsistencies (2)
- Generally inconsistent (1)

Simplification

1. What style of simplifying key business processes have we adopted (evolutionary or revolutionary); is this consistent with the business strategy; and is this appropriate to our competitive needs? (simplification and style)

- Very appropriate indeed (3)
- Appropriate, approximately (2)
- Inappropriate (1)

2. How can quality management be simplified wherever possible to add more value at least cost? (simplification and quality)

– Doesn't need simplifying at all (3)
– Requires modest simplification (2)
– Requires a lot of simplification (1)

3. Should our cost management processes be simplified to generate greater visibility for the areas of highest and possibly unnecessary cost? (simplification and costs)

– No simplification needed (3)
– Some simplification needed (2)
– A lot of simplification needed (1)

4. Can our overall skills base be simplified significantly (for instance, by multi-skilling)? (simplification and skills)

– No call for simplifying skills (3)
– Possible benefits for simplification (not currently addressed) (2)
– Lots of benefits from simplification (not currently addressed) (1)

5. Is the business strategy overly complex and therefore inviting of simplification? (simplification and strategy)

– No need for simplification (3)
– Some need for simplification and refocusing (2)
– Major need for simplification and refocusing (1)

Strategy

1. Do we have a strategy for quality management in terms of objectives and outputs, and also in having a strategy for implementation? (strategy and quality)

– Clear strategy exists (3)
– Strategy is partial and incomplete (2)
– No real strategy exists (1)

2. Are cost management efforts always aimed at managing costs strategically rather than to achieve merely short-term temporary and localized cost reduction? (strategy and costs)

– Costs are managed strategically as a general rule (3)

- Only sometimes are costs managed strategically (2)
- Costs are rarely (if ever) managed strategically (1)

3. Does the strategy for developing organizational skills dovetail neatly into the business strategy (for instance, through linking critical success factors)? (strategy and skills)

- Dovetails neatly (3)
- Some links exist but these are tenuous in part (2)
- No real links (1)

4. Is there a clear strategy for implementing a desired shift in management style or in sustaining a preferred style? (strategy and style)

- A clear strategy exists (3)
- A partial strategy exists (2)
- No real strategy exists (1)

5. Are efforts at simplifying the business bound together within a coherent strategy? (strategy and simplification)

- Simplification strategy exists (3)
- Some parts of a strategy exist (2)
- No real strategy exists (1)

Evaluating your scores

Score 30–45: You have clearly a long way to go in enhancing organization capability.

Score 45–60: Although there are many areas for improvement, you are starting from a basis of some capabilities being in place and reinforcing others.

Score 60–75: You are relatively well placed to create and sustain improvements in organizational capability and performance.

Score 75–90: Congratulations! Most of the building blocks are in place for you now to reap the benefits of strong, organizational capability through business performance.

Final task

Now identify *three areas* for improving organizational capability that are likely to have greatest impact on business performance. What performance improvements could you expect to achieve:

- Within six months?
- Within eighteen months?
- Within three years?

8.4 Conclusions

In this chapter we learned how Interspace Corporation has sought to transform its capability and performance via a learning process. This involved viewing business issues in a cross-functional and strategic way, including those that are involved in shifting the organization from one state to another.

In the Interspace case, and in devising your own analysis, we were effectively considering a relatively new area of strategy: *organizational strategy*. HR strategy, IT strategy and operations strategy are all well recognised by management thinkers, and so is organizational change. *Organizational strategy*, however, gives a new and more useful focus to mobilizing people, processes and power bases for strategic change. Organizational strategy (as illustrated in the Interspace case) enables both capability and performance to be addressed by considering people and processes in unison.

9
Towards personal strategic learning

9.1 Making strategic learning happen – for you

Much of this book has focused on how teams of managers and the wider organization can share strategic learning, but it is equally applicable to issues that are specific to the individual. By applying strategic learning to your own role there are additional insights that can be gained which you are now invited to explore. Although this takes us into, perhaps, less glamorous territory relative to the four core cases in Chapters 5–8, it may be of more immediate, personal importance.

This aim can be achieved via two main thrusts:

– to enable you to understand more about your *current position* and how to reshape this to advantage
– to explore *where* you might wish to be at future stages in your career, and *how* you might achieve that as part of a longer-term strategy.

This involves taking an assessment of your own capability and potential to see what your existing position is, what your options are, and how you might implement these options. It also involves examining your underlying values as these can help steer you away from apparently attractive career choices that may clash with your more fundamental desires and expectations. In effect, it involves looking at yourself as a business that is subject to personal, yet strategic change.

We shall achieve this together by looking at the following key questions:

1. What business are you in?
2. What are your sources of personal competitive advantage?
3. Do you have a strategy for your career?
4. How will you implement the transition?

These key questions are represented pictorially in Figure 9.1.

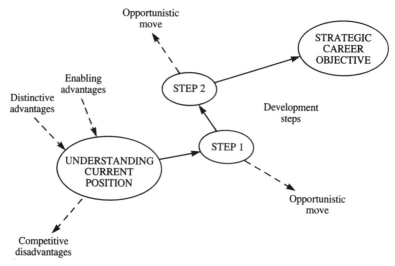

Figure 9.1   Steering your future via strategic learning

Figure 9.1 begins with understanding your current position. This involves identifying both your 'enabling advantages' (for instance, core functional skills) as well as your distinctive advantage (for example, political skills or vision). It also requires analysis of your personal competitive disadvantages. It then explores what your strategic career objective might be. Depending upon the point you have already reached in your career and aspirations, this might have a 3–5 year time-scale, or possibly even longer.

A short illustration might help at this juncture. For instance, after I qualified as an accountant, I set my strategic career objective as being a move into management consulting. In order to achieve this objective I had two roles: one in a very large company, and one in a medium-sized company – one a staff role and one in a line role.

Although strategies for career development may *emerge* as opposed to being *deliberate* (again see Figure 9.1) opportunistic moves may become career culs-de-sac. For instance, when I joined a medium-sized company, the experience gained was invaluable through having a senior position at an early age, but in looking for my next role no one outside the industry had even heard of that company! (The company was a specialist niche in the retail industry.)

9.2 What business are you in?

When defining your organizational role, it is rarely self-evident as to 'what business you are in'. Although many roles are relatively fluid, it is still necessary to have a clear understanding of what is (or should be) at the core of this role.

The traditional way of defining roles – for instance, in terms of defining your key, fixed responsibilities – is less relevant in an environment of continual change, which most managers now find themselves facing. Nevertheless, even in a fluid environment it is essential to understand how you currently *add value* to the organization and how you could *add more*. This 'added value' test is extremely useful as it reinforces activities that you should be doing, and questions activities of a less valuable or more dubious nature.

For instance, in an ideal world a financial director might add value by:

– providing input into the strategic decision-making process;
– providing consultancy advice on key business issues;
– suggesting new areas for business development;
– keeping track of financial performance;
– interpreting this performance so that operational managers can take rapid corrective action;
– providing internal and external confidence in the business;
– satisfying regulatory requirements so that the business can continue to trade;
– optimizing the development of the company's financial resources – long and short term;
– promoting a cost-aware culture;
– helping avoid both strategic and tactical blunders;
– developing staff so that they understand the business and are able to communicate (without unnecessary mystique) to other departments.

Some of the above elements will not appear to be particularly 'new'. However, some finance directors may place much emphasis on some areas, but less on others. For instance, many financial directors may not see it as their role to be suggesting new areas for business development; or they may see this as incidental. This may be partly related to the role expectations set by his or her discipline, and partly by the organization. Yet a financial director may be particularly well-placed to identify possible profit-making opportunities.

In addition, he or she may not see the position as a consultancy role. More typically, the financial director's function may be seen as a 'controlling role', hardly conducive to have a consultancy style. Further, the burden of regulatory requirements may drive out other value-adding activities. This may be even though this adds value purely via keeping the organization in business.

A typical pattern is thus one where the individual – like many businesses – lacks a clear focus on 'what business he or she is in' and also 'where he or she can add most value'. This lack of focus means that, while you are able to satisfy more routine demands, there is an acute lack of time and energy to deviate to activities of a more strategic nature where you may add more value. As a result, you may begin to lack personal competitive advantage and thus be a 'me-too' player in the organization.

Exercise 9.1 (10 minutes)

What value do you generate in your own role and in what key processes? How can you reshape your role to add more value, and possibly *distinctive value*? What does this suggest about how you can develop your personal competitive advantage?

Following the above exercise you may have identified some key shifts in what you do, and also how it is prioritized. In order to achieve these shifts in 'how I do things around here', you may need to programme how you can *stop doing* things that do not add value and *start doing* new things that add very high value.

Case study 9.1

In the course of a J. Lyons General Management programme, the sales manager of a major business unit decided to examine what his key activities were, and also how much time and effort he spent on them. His analysis suggested he was working a 55-hour week, which made him increasingly unpopular with his family.

Although about 40 per cent of his time was devoted to 'customer-related issues', nearly 75 per cent of these could be related to dealing with quality problems of a wider nature beyond his own area of responsibility. Following this realization he determined that he would stop doing quality-chasing for others and would instead flag these problems as a major issue for senior management.

The rest of the sales manager's analysis of how he spent his time was also of interest. The total picture looked as follows:

	Hours/week	%
Customer-related issues (of which three-quarters was spent on quality-chasing)	22	40
Travel to visit customers	19	34
Personal contact time with customers	5	9
Telephone contact time with customers	2	4
Administration	7	13
Total	55	100

Notice the high proportion of time spent chasing quality problems (30 per cent) and on administration (13 per cent): 53 per cent in total. Also, look at the low amount of time spent in personal and telephone contact: 13 per cent.

Besides the shift out of quality-chasing work the sales manager also looked carefully at his travel time. Apparently several of his customers were in central London. Currently he spent 6 hours a week driving down the motorway to London when he could have gone by train. At a stroke, he was therefore able to spend this wasted travel time to remove most of his administration time, freeing up 10 per cent of his total time for better use. He then opted to spend half of this 'saved' time on more effective planning of his marketing and sales strategy – something he had previously done informally.

The above study graphically highlights how asking the question 'How am I adding value?' can provoke some major changes in how a manager executes his or her role and in personal effectiveness. Challenging how you spend your time and with what added value should be habitual. Continual reflection on how you add or do not add value thereby leads to sustained, personal competitive advantage.

One of the most difficult parts of all, however, is to stop doing things that actually *destroy value*. If we return to our notional case of the financial director, one can think of a number of ways in which he or she may destroy value, for example by:

- adopting an excessively tight approach to financial controls which results in gross inflexibility;
- imposing over-complex financial controls, for instance, in authorizing investment or costs;
- slowing down the decision-making process to a snail's pace;
- intimidating champions of new and valuable ideas;
- adopting a policing rather than a consulting role – in its extreme form, giving managers the freedom to make major technical, financial blunders and then punishing them for not knowing what they should have done;

and so on ...

The next exercise gives you the opportunity to reflect on those areas in which you may be destroying value.

Exercise 9.2 (5 minutes)

How are you inadvertently destroying value in your organization? What causes you to do this? Is it your personal or professional style, or is this the way people customarily behave in the organization? Is it because your role overlaps with that of other managers or because tensions and conflicts are allowed to get out of hand?

An honest response to the above exercise should highlight at least one, and possibly several, areas where you are destroying value. The incidence of value destruction may be rife in the organization. This helps to explain why, when a well-focused 10–20 per cent reduction in managers within an organization is coupled with a shift in style and refocusing of activities, little seems to suffer.

The analysis of how you create and destroy value in the organization leads us to the next topic: looking at your personal competitive advantage.

9.3 What are your sources of personal competitive advantage?

Although the idea of competitive advantage is by now widely spread in management thinking, it has yet to crystallize in how individual managers think about their personal capability. Over the past few years much energy has been expended identifying and seeking to develop management competences. But many of these initiatives have absorbed a great deal of analysis while the outputs have been slow to arrive, often cumbersome and usually cluttered.

Effective management behaviour is complex, but there may be a relatively small number of key ingredients that offer personal, competitive advantage. These key ingredients may account for 80 per cent of what may be a distinctive (as opposed to a mediocre) performance, yet account for only 20 per cent (Pareto) of possible competences.

For instance, many managers contemplate, at some stage in their careers, 'going independent as a management consultant'. They may (erroneously) believe that the most critical competences will be found in the area of functional skills and excellence. However, from a *customer's point of view*, these competences are often regarded as merely getting the player into the game – they are purely *enabling*.

Some critical personal competences to become a successful, independent management consultant are as follows:

1. *Holistic vision*: being able to see problems holistically – across functions, in their historical and political context.
2. *Implementation focus*: understanding the issues associated with implementing change to resolve these problems, and also to facilitate this change in addition to having 'expert skills'.
3. *Distinctive, interrelated skills*: having a core of well-honed skills which form a *distinctive cluster* – i.e. they form part of a distinctive set.
4. *Presentation of self*: as an independent consultant you would need to have, or develop, some sense of personal distinctiveness which fits your personal style and target clients. This might embrace, for instance,

becoming an acknowledged expert in the field in the public domain, finely honing your interpersonal skills and being flexible to tackle 'how you come over' to match individual client styles.

5. *Networking*: the ability to gather information and build relationships is crucial in order to help get people to come to you with their problems, as opposed to you chasing around to find them with their problems.

6. *Flexibility*: in order to provide a preferred alternative to the larger consulting firms you would need to develop flexibility to be able to respond in a more relevant and rapid mode.

Although some of these skills overlap with ones sought by larger consulting firms, they differ in key respects – for instance, in the breadth of skills needed, the emphasis on networking and also on flexibility. Some of these key competences may be important to the line manager as well as to external or internal consultants, albeit with a differing mix.

You may wish to reflect now about how your own enabling competences differ from your (possibly) distinctive competences. Try the next exercise:

Exercise 9.3   Understanding your personal competitive advantage (20 minutes)

1. What are the sources of personal competitive advantage, which *enable* you to execute your role competently, for instance, in your:

   - functional skills?
   - knowledge of how the business works?
   - interpersonal skills?
   - project/management skills?
   - skills in planning and controlling resources?
   - communication skills?

2. What are your sources of personal competitive advantage which give you a distinctive capability, for instance, in your:

   - ability to look at problems cross-functionally and to analyse these strategically?
   - leading-edge knowledge base (and one which is particularly relevant to resolving key business problems)?
   - leadership ability and strategic vision?
   - competence in facilitating change?
   - knowledge of the industry, your customers, competitors, suppliers, etc.?
   - international experience and fluency in particular languages and cultures?
   - unusually strong network of relationships giving you the capacity to influence decisions and thinking at senior management level?

3. What are your key sources of personal *competitive disadvantage*? For instance, do you have:

- specific skills where you are weak in areas that are regarded as fundamental by the customers who in effect buy your services?
- single-functional vision?
- major knowledge gaps – for instance, in marketing, IT or finance?
- lack of exposure to how things are done elsewhere in the organization?
- low awareness of how other companies work, especially in your field of expertise?
- lack of experience of front-line management (for advisory staff who may not appreciate the pressures that line managers often face)?
- acute aversion to risk and to making errors?
- a tendency to deny or oversimplify problems?
- an apparent inability to plan ahead longer than a few months?

Having worked through these questions using the various points as a checklist, you may now be in a better position to get some fix on 'where you are now'. These prompts may have highlighted some competitive advantages that enable you to do your role effectively, and may have suggested some areas in which you have a *distinctive* advantage.

They may also have pinpointed areas of personal, competitive disadvantage. Just one of these areas of disadvantage may in effect eliminate you for significant, upward or horizontal career progression. For instance, your experience base may be too narrow if you have spent a long time in a single function or area of the business; or you may have had a succession of roles that were not very demanding and would therefore not have prepared you for the quantum leap to a general management role, or to head up a significant functional area. For organizations that are more process-based or project-based, personal competitive disadvantage can be equally debilitating.

Outputs from these exercises now help you to build (or adapt) your strategy for career development.

9.4 Do you have a strategy for your career?

Based on my contact with a large number of managers at both senior and middle levels, it would appear that relatively few individuals have formulated a clearly considered career strategy. This situation is beginning to change, partly due to the major restructurings of the early 1990s. These have made many managers reflect on where their career paths are heading at greater length, although often in an all-structured way. For many, this chapter may therefore provide the first formal opportunity to explore, in a structured way, your career options. This involves looking at how these options fit with your personal competitive advantages, your development opportunities and your personal values. This process will also help those (probably few) managers who have given this topic considerable thought with an opportunity to refine and possibly refocus their strategy.

Before we begin, it is advisable to lift some possible constraints. Not all managers may see that they have a need for a career strategy, however. A common objection to having a strategy for your career was put to me by a National Health Service manager:

> I hear what you say, but I have survived very well not having a career strategy. I have found it possible to find new opportunities to stimulate me every couple of years. By having a career strategy you would have to rule out all kinds of interesting opportunities.

In this case, having a loose career strategy obviously worked for this particular manager. However, he might well have had a lucky run in the past – these opportunities happened to add to his experience and skills without leaving him in a career rut. Other managers may not be always so fortunate when embarking on a purely opportunistic career. Arguably, given the state of flux in Britain's National Health Service, what worked in the past might prove to be a very poor guide to what will work in the future.

Earlier in this chapter, within Figure 9.1, we mentioned that development opportunities may occur which lead roughly (although rarely explicitly) in the direction of the career objective. However, where a manager decides on an opportunistic route, it can end up being a cul-de-sac. The 'once-in-a-lifetime' experience may turn rapidly into a nightmare. Once again, this invites a personal illustration with which many managers will empathize.

During the middle of my own career, I confess to making one such mistake. I joined an organization to perform a role which, on the surface, had exact fit to my strategic career objective in terms of type of work, type of company, geographical location, seniority and package, immediate boss, etc. At the time I felt some concerns about the move. For instance, during the interviews my future employers seemed very keen on my joining the company. Subsequently there seemed to be an unreasonably long delay in offering me the position. I began to wonder what was happening behind the scenes? Did this role really exist? And if it did, what politics were going on to make this role such an evident football? Was I suffering from corporate paranoia, or were my natural instincts telling me something I would be unwise to ignore?

There also seemed to be a degree of confusion during my interview: could I please wait while they dragged a senior consultant away from finalizing a report (which looked like a last-minute panic) to talk to me? Was this a sign that this consulting firm had a very much less-organized style to the one I was accustomed to? You may recognize these symptoms from some of your own career move experiences.

Like many other managers, I had these concerns but they became dampened by what seemed to be the obvious strategic fit of this move, not to mention dissatisfaction with where I was now. Sometimes, however, it pays to listen to the stomach rather than the heart or even the head in assessing a new role. In my case it was not long – two to three months – before the gap between my job aspirations and the organizational reality which I faced in the new role was fully evident. Not only was the nature of the role different to what I had been led to believe, the consulting work actually being done was a very different mix and the business unit lacked the critical skills to compete in the market. Yet on the surface, all of these things seemed to have been in place.

After six months, when I had received no response to my protestations about false expectations being raised, I resigned. The comment from a senior manager in the organization was interesting:

> But Tony, you didn't come to tell us that you were so discontented – we had no inkling that you were about to resign. And we just put you as project leader of a major client review....

You may be interested to hear what happened subsequently. Two years after I had left, the business unit had been effectively dissolved following the early onset of recession. The heroic strategy of the business unit to grow into an 'attractive' consulting niche where it had little real competitive advantage was a total failure. This was after wave after wave of reorganizations and redundancies, coupled with redeployment. The lessons of this experience are several:

1. Never let yourself be talked into a career move of dubious benefit while under the influence of profound (but possibly temporary) dissatisfaction with 'where you are now'.
2. If you do make a career mistake, it is often better to pull the rug quickly rather than to let it drag on. Very quickly your new organization will bleat loudly that you haven't really tried hard and for long enough. You may also feel increasingly committed even though your commitment is to the wrong thing.
3. When moving organizations in the same industry, never assume that the culture and style of working will be more or less the same – it could be radically different in subtle ways that seem arbitrary and often counter-productive.
4. Sometimes it is better to defer a career move so that you can take a bigger

step rather than accept something that may seem to have some fit but may well be a compromise.

5. Regardless of any misfit, always see what you can salvage out of a move of this kind – in terms of experience, skills, development and personal contacts. In this particular case, the one year I spent was used to great value in developing the skills to become an independent strategy consultant.

Although this discussion has focused primarily on very major, cross-organization moves, similar lessons can be applied to moves within the same organization.

Exercise 9.4 Reflecting on a past career move (10 minutes)

For one career move made either within your existing organization or in moving between organizations in the past:

1. To what extent was this part of a longer-term career strategy, or was it essentially opportunistic?
2. Did this matter either way? What were the benefits, costs, risks?
3. What options did this particular career step open up, for instance, in future career moves?
4. How did it help you develop relative to what you expected?
5. If you were to go back in time, and repeat the experience, what things (if any) would you have done differently?

Obviously, your own organization may have played a role in shaping this move, if it was an internal role. This raises the whole issue of what to do when a senior manager approaches you with 'the offer you can't refuse'. In many organizations it is still expected by managers, especially at middle levels, that 'if they ask you to do something, you do it'. Yet you may even not be competent to do it. A not uncommon scenario is for subtle (or less subtle) psychological pressure to be brought to bear. For instance, at the age of 25, I was asked to apply for a senior finance job in the Far East, when I wanted a corporate planning job at Group Centre of a major company. The response was:

> But Tony, it really is a very nice place, you can take your family – it is hot and the pay is good. And remember, we won't forget you, as you will still be on London's books.

(My boss had evidently forgotten, in extolling the virtues of this particular country, that I had been there on business two months' earlier. He had also forgotten that my wife was at university in the UK and that I had, after all, wanted a job at the Centre precisely so that I wouldn't be forgotten at such an early juncture by London!)

This may seem an extreme example, but it does highlight how critical it is for the individual to own his or her career.

This leads on to thinking strategically about different kinds of future strategic career options. Figure 9.2 looks at two key variables: the degree of shift in style versus role. (Incidentally, the idea for this grid came from other strategic tools, especially the analysis of existing versus new products and markets when comparing new business development opportunities.)

The figure shows some examples of role moves to give some idea of how radical the shifts are. For instance, a move within a similar functional role in the same organizational unit will be at the bottom left-hand corner of the matrix. A promotion in the same organization within function may be mid-way, but to the left. However, a promotion into general management will be to the very centre. This may involve a significantly different *style* of managing.

Continuing this analysis, a move to another organization could involve a different or possibly very different style from what you have been accustomed to. A move from a function to a general management role across organizations could be mid-way up and to the right. Stretching these options even further, a first experience in general management involving at

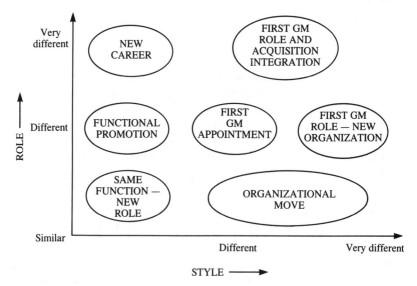

Figure 9.2 Evaluating the impact of career options

the same time the integration of an acquisition, or say a turnaround job, would be to the far, top-right corner. Many Groups in the past saw their 'bright young things' (possibly with an MBA or accounting qualification) going in at the deep end to integrate a new business. Sometimes this works, and sometimes it doesn't – at any rate it is high risk. My opening case in Chapter 1, Nebula International, falls into this category.

Finally, a new career altogether might involve a very different role and a similar or different style. For instance, someone moving from line management into consulting or from consulting, into a more academic role, may find this a very different career. Yet each crossing of a boundary may seem to be quite a small step, until afterwards. These positionings are illustrative, rather than definitive – you will need to interpret the position on a case-by-case basis.

It is now appropriate to look at your own longer-term career strategy, and consider how you will manage your career transitions, via the exercise presented below. We have already covered some of the key ingredients for this exercise, such as understanding how you add or destroy value in your current role, and also understanding your personal, competitive advantage. This defines your *current position.*

In the exercise, you should try to picture yourself at some *future* point in your career. This might be three, five or possibly eight years into the future, depending on how far you have progressed into your career and what your personal and organizational context suggests are options. For instance, if you are a 'fast mover' and are at an early stage in your career, you may wish to look at a three-year horizon within your current organization, possibly alongside some five-year options outside it. If you are somewhere on a career plateau, then you may need to begin to think about the possibilities of a new career in, say, five or eight years' time. This assumes a relatively stable environment. Or, if the organization faces rapid change, it may be sensible to collapse these time-scales and think about embarking on a new career strategy within one to two years, or less.

Now, try to answer the questions in the following exercise, as they are important. Don't just skim on to the next section, but spend 20–30 minutes pondering your options. Return to these questions when next you are involved in a traffic jam or are otherwise immobilized. Use your 'dead time' to advantage by reflecting strategically on your career.

Exercise 9.5 Setting a personal career strategy (20–30 minutes)

1. How is your own organization changing and developing over the time-scale of your career strategy?
2. How do these changes and developments fit your current capabilities and those that you want to develop?
3. What specific opportunities and threats may be posed to your career within the organization? (Try to think not just short term, but about longer-term opportunities and threats.)
4. What does your analysis of your personal competitive advantage suggest in the kind of opportunities elsewhere that may fit your capabilities?
5. How do these relate to your style of working, personal values and personal life generally – including long-buried aspirations – which you might like (still) to fulfil?
6. What competences would you need to develop to enhance your career either through options (a) internally within the organization, (b) externally, i.e. elsewhere?
7. How difficult would it be to develop these competences – and within sufficient time to be able to exploit the opportunity in question?
8. What could go wrong with a particular career option? How could you find out more in order to assess the risks, and to gain more flexibility should these risks crystallize?
9. How do these options compare with that of following your existing or similar career path, while making the very best of what you already have?
10. If you consider that you have already fulfilled your career strategy, what new challenges do you feel you might now fruitfully seek?

This exercise parallels earlier ones in the book which involved generating and assessing strategic options at the business level. It involves looking at your objectives and values, doing internal and external analysis, and analysing your competitive position. It includes evaluating the key opportunities and threats and also indicates how easy or difficult it will be to implement a number of strategic options, and with what results. In fact, it is one of the crimes of modern business thinking that 'strategy' has become associated primarily (if not exclusively) with strategy at the corporate or business levels rather than at the personal level. For the individual manager it can yield some quite powerful and immediate insights.

As a result of the above exercise, you may now have gained insights similar to those listed below.

1. While you have enjoyed working in your current organization, at best it offers your career development a quiet cul-de-sac. At worst, this comfortable position may evaporate owing to pending organizational change.

2. A new opportunity may have suggested itself either through a possible internal or external move, but when subjected to closer scrutiny it does not really fit with your underlying aims, abilities or values.

3. For some time you have considered the idea of a different career, but now you realize that you must make the jump soon or you may begin to appreciate how difficult such a move might be and decide to freeze the idea.

4. You may have come to the conclusion that, inadvertently, you are in danger of becoming stuck in a particular career rut, perhaps within a particular function. It may now be time to make active steps towards, for instance, securing a general management position.

Following this exploration of your career options, let us now turn to the issue of managing career transitions.

9.5 How will you implement the transition?

Implementing a career strategy or a more tactical career move may give rise to the problem of managing a career transition. A career transition involves a major personal change. This change may go through a cycle of:

- *expectation-building*: often of the exciting opportunities offered by the change;
- *disappointment*: when these expectations are partially met, or are dashed;
- *adaptation*: to the new environment, through modifying your style;
- *consolidation*: of your new role, by routinizing the things that are working.

This cycle can be protracted in duration, especially if you have not identified the transition explicitly as a consensus learning process.

So how is it possible to manage career transition as a learning process? Let us begin by re-examining a past experience where you were involved in a significant career transition.

Exercise 9.6 (10 minutes)

Think back to a major career transition that you have gone through in the past.

1. Was this a success or a failure, or very much a mixed picture?
2. To what extent was this outcome affected by whether you saw this transition *explicitly* as a learning process?
3. With hindsight, what would you have done differently in managing this career transition?
4. What lessons can you glean for future or current career transitions?

continued

In answering this question there may be issues you wish to consider, for instance:

- Did you understand the degree to which you saw the transition as a major discontinuity requiring different skills and recipes from those that had worked well in past roles?
- Did you avoid premature action to deliver quick results in the interest of performing a fuller diagnosis of the issues surrounding your new role?
- Did you get a clear picture of any stakeholders who might impact on these issues, and how you might influence them?
- Did you then manage expectations of these stakeholders on what you will deliver, when, and with what style?

A useful method of picturing the key factors impacting on the transition is by using *force-field analysis*:

First, define the key forces that will allow you to make an effective career transition (the 'enabling forces'). Second, define the key forces that will constrain them (the 'constraining forces'). Third, evaluate the relative strength or importance of each of these forces – for instance, as 'high', 'medium' or 'low'.

Once you have reached this point you can draw up a rough force-field analysis picture. As an illustration, Figure 9.3 depicts one for my own career: a move from being a consultant in a large consulting firm to being a researcher (part-time) at a business school. You will need to avoid skipping over the illustration as it paves the way for you to use this tool within your next exercise.

At the time I saw this particular transition as one that was relatively easy to make. I viewed this change as being 'more of the same' – just in a slightly different organization – but Figure 9.3 reveals a very different picture.

1. Although I had identified the objective of my (research) task clearly, I had little detailed idea of what was involved in actually achieving it.
2. Despite being very committed to the task and having strong professorial support, my mindset clashed with that required to do research. Also my position in the organization was peripheral and I lacked the political resources to get things done in mobilizing the research programme. I was also dependent on relatively short-term funding. This put pressure on me to achieve very rapid results, without regard for culture and style differences.
3. Finally, and most dangerously of all, I had misplaced confidence in my own skills. Instead of being strong – relative to the research task – they were actually weak. This is not uncommon in many major career transitions, and this can result in total, transition failure.

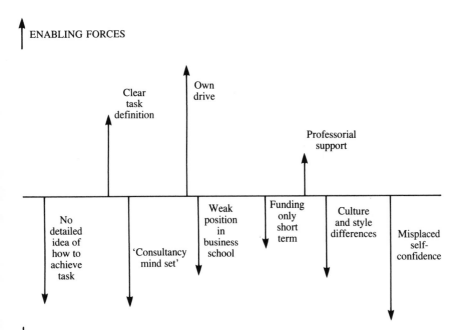

ENABLING FORCES

CONSTRAINING FORCES

Figure 9.3   A force-field analysis of a past career transition

You will see at a glance that this transition seemed to be doomed to failure. Indeed, during the early and middle phases the transition nearly ended that way. However, over a period of 18 months, it proved possible to reshape the transition, as shown in Figure 9.4.

Compare the differences between Figures 9.3 and 9.4: a number of constraining forces have been reduced (for instance, the impact of my consultancy mindset has diluted), or have actually been reversed to become enabling forces. For instance, after strong criticism, which I received at a research presentation (probably the intellectual equivalent of an SAS attack), I realized that my previous self-confidence was misplaced. Also I took on board (during the adaptation phase) a sound methodology, which was also accompanied by increased professorial support. My role at the business school was also refocused to untangle some of the role conflict and resulting 'weak position' shown in Figure 9.3. This shift also identifies how *shock* can be an important jolt to begin strategic learning.

The lessons from this experience are that it is extremely useful to draw up a formal picture of the forces enabling and constraining effective career

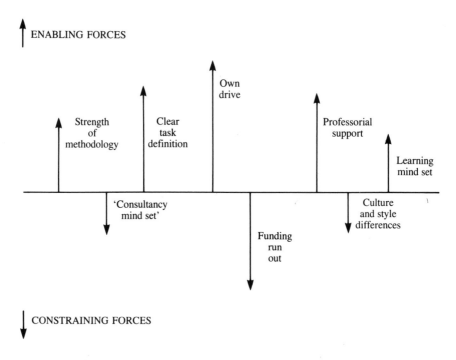

ENABLING FORCES

Own
drive

Strength   Clear   Professorial
of   task   support
methodology   definition

Learning
mind set

'Consultancy   Culture
mind set'   and style
                                                      differences

Funding
run
out

CONSTRAINING FORCES

Figure 9.4 A reshaped force-field analysis of a career transition

transitions. This can be done relatively quickly (in about 5–10 minutes) using force-field analysis. Even if your analysis falls short of drawing up a formal force-field analysis diagram, separating out the enabling and constraining forces provides a way of sensing where the most vulnerable parts of the transition process are.

Having been patient in following this illustration, you should now be in a good position to explore one of your own career transitions using force-field analysis. Here you have two main choices. You may either:

(a) choose a transition that you are going through at the moment or will probably be going through in the near future; or

(b) choose a transition that you have gone through in the past.

Exercise 9.7 Exploring the enabling and constraining forces of a career transition (10 minutes)

For either (a) a current or potential career transition, or (b) a past career transition:

1. Can you identify the key forces that would enable the career transition to be achieved effectively?
2. Can you identify the key forces that would constrain the career transition to be achieved effectively?
3. Are any of these forces likely to have a 'high', 'medium' or 'low' impact in achieving an effective transition?
4. If the transition is one that occurred in the past, how might you have reshaped these forces to make the process of transition more effective?
5. If the transition is a current, or potential one, how might you now reshape these forces to make the process of transition more effective?

Note: for the reshaping process, give considerable thought to new forces or influences that you can bring into play.

This now concludes our discussion of how a career strategy can be both developed and implemented effectively. It also leads us to our key conclusions in achieving personal, strategic learning.

9.6 Conclusions

In this chapter I have shown how strategic learning can be of continual relevance in shaping your personal career. Strategic learning is not, therefore, something that just happens in the strategic clouds, but is a very practical and personally relevant discipline. This can be achieved by:

- thinking hard about career moves, not merely in terms of the value of the immediate move, but also the value of things it might lead to, and also things it might preclude;
- being continuously aware of whether and how you are adding concrete value to the organization;
- avoiding destroying value in your role (at all costs) even if this means fighting against organizational style;
- understanding what your key sources of personal competitive advantage are and continually building on these (particularly your distinctive ones);
- seeing your learning capability as a core area of competitive advantage;
- thinking about the fit of your bundle of personal competitive advantages and disadvantages against your current and potential roles;
- having a broad strategy for developing your own career;

- screening new career opportunities against this strategy – and taking notice of possible areas of mismatch rather than playing these down;
- assessing very carefully the risks associated with career diversification and reflecting these in your transition plans;
- treating career transitions as a key application for strategic learning;
- using force-field analysis to understand the problems of transition and reshaping your approach to help make the transition quickly and effectively.

In any organization you will have some personal competitive advantages and disadvantages, career opportunities and threats. It seems a very wise move to manage these as part of a career strategy, continually being reshaped through learning.

PART FOUR
A SYNTHESIS

10
Conclusion

10.1 Introduction

In this concluding chapter we gain an overview of strategic learning and re-examine the learning traps that threaten its success. We then look at how strategic learning can be sustained before considering the value that strategic learning can bring.

10.2 The learning traps

The cases of Shell, Dowty Communications and Mercury Messaging, and the composite case of Interspace, all highlighted some key benefits of strategic learning. In these cases strategic learning helped to:

- evaluate key sources of uncertainty, discontinuity and change in the external environment;
- create strategic plans which reflect the knowledge, intuition and judgement of many managers in the organization, and not just a select few;
- make implementation plans which take into account explicitly the less obvious but crucial factors that might enable or constrain change;
- shift organizational capability and improve business performance.

These applications of strategic learning form a series of loops (the three S's), as seen in Figure 10.1:

- scenario analysis
- strategy-making
- steering implementation.

These loops overlap because each phase requires input from a previous one. Also, Figure 10.1 highlights how scenario analysis can be used not merely for strategy-making but also for steering implementation. For instance, a scenario can be drawn up for how a major organizational change may materialize based on (a) everything falling neatly into place versus (b) progress being impeded by stakeholders against the change. Organizational

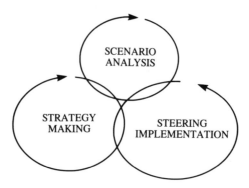

Figure 10.1 Loops of strategic learning: the three S's

scenarios can be used to test the feasibility of making major change work or to test organizational strategy for key events that may disrupt its course. Often there are abrupt (or sometimes predictable) changes in leadership, and thus of style.

We have also seen throughout the book that it is not always straightforward to implement strategic learning effectively. Strategic learning needs to avoid a number of traps in order to achieve and sustain benefits. These can be summarized as:

1. *The 'brain power trap':* learning being viewed as purely an intellectual or cognitive issue, one that is dissociated from behaviour, attitudes and values (which it most clearly is not).
2. *The 'training trap':* learning being seen as a peripheral issue, a 'nice to do' – one that is associated with more formal training and development programmes rather than being at the core of competitive advantage.
3. *The 'commitment trap':* the main drive for learning becomes one primarily of intellectual or social stimulation rather than one of securing tangible business or other benefit. Once the learning goal is fulfilled, there is inadequate commitment to pursue action objectives.
4. *The 'denial trap':* managers' openness to exposing the truth is severely limited by resistance to admit to errors or embarrassments.

Each of these traps can be dealt with, but in different ways. The 'brain power trap' is perhaps more difficult to address – at least in our Western culture. Much of Western management thinking (at least pre-1980) seems to be based upon heroic rationalism, which held that if only we could be more rational, more clever, all of our business and organizational problems would simply dissolve. Realizing that learning involves uprooting behaviours and attitudes – and also nudging some deeper-seated values – is something that is quite new to many of us.

The 'training trap' can be addressed by making the distinction between strategic, organizational and personal development much more blurred than in the past. The focus can be shifted from 'pure training' to 'learning, development and change' and by bringing in senior managers to become integral with the learning process. Many leading UK companies are now seeking to make these shifts but are, as yet (at 1993), at an early stage of experimentation.

The 'commitment trap' needs a number of measures. If leadership really immerses itself in the learning process then there is a much greater change of building commitment to achieve. It is a surprise that leaders do not often see learning as a core part of their role: learning and leadership are natural allies. Not only should leaders excel in strategic learning (and some do), but they should also be skilled in setting a climate for learning – and orchestrating it.

Finally, managing the 'denial trap' is a continuous and possibly an endless process. Where managers are involved in managing complex business systems there is *always the opportunity* to blame some part of the system for defect or error. Often that part of the system was not designed to handle a non-routine demand and is insufficiently flexible to cope. Blaming the system will result in no change. Pulling it apart and reassembling it to become more flexible is much more difficult and requires a lot more patience.

In the remainder of this chapter we review how strategic learning fits within management practice generally, and also draw some lessons for future development. First, let us turn to sustaining development and enhancing strategic learning.

10.3 Sustaining and enhancing strategic learning

Strategic learning is not easy to sustain and requires openness, tenacity and time to bear fruit. It can only become effective through practice, patience and persistence. The reason why many attempts at strategic learning fail or droop is often because managers' time horizons are too short to give it critical mass and momentum. (This has been called, perhaps unfairly to gerbils, the GM or Gerbil Management syndrome – as many gerbils seem to have a longer attention span than some managers.) Managers' horizons of patience are often measured in hours and days, when often weeks and months are required.

The dimensions of strategic learning can now be usefully represented in

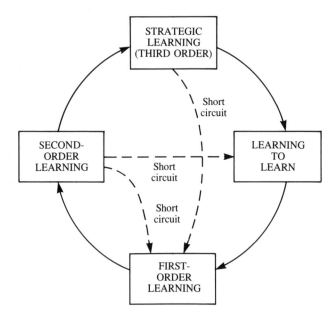

Figure 10.2   Completing the strategic learning cycle

Figure 10.2. First-order learning is associated with achieving a particular given task more efficiently than in the past. Second-order learning occurs when a task is attempted in a new way, in order to achieve its goal more effectively.

First-order learning thus involve tasks which involve business issues that are likely to be relatively simple. Second-order learning is different because of the increased *complexity* of the tasks involved and the complexity of the associated learning process.

Strategic learning involves learning how more complex business content and management process issues can be analysed and evaluated at the same time. This much more complex learning involves not merely tackling an existing task or problem in a new way (second-order learning) but typically a *redefinition of the original problem and process*. Potentially this may involve relating the problem to even larger and possibly more complex problems (thus 'chunking' the problem), or breaking it down into sub-problems.

Applications of strategic learning include scenario analysis, strategy development, implementing change and personal career development, which all involve *learning to learn*. The barriers to open learning escalate as we move from first- to second-order learning, and then to third-order strategic learning.

The cycle depicted in Figure 10.2 is liable to short circuit at a number of points. For instance, this may happen either at the first- or second-order level. Even where a degree of strategic learning is achieved, managers may then fail to learn how to sustain and enhance that strategic learning (learning to learn).

Argyris[1] documented many ways in which learning (and learning to learn) becomes blocked when managers use defensive routines. This raises the issue as to what measures are available to counter defensive reactions, and how these can deal with counter-activities. Measures to promote open learning may include:

- a willingness to explore *power relationships as* well as more 'content' issues in the management process, particularly through analysing key stakeholders[2]
- a more open, flexible *structure* through which learning can be disseminated more freely
- *rewards* and *recognition* processes and controls to reinforce open learning
- learning *routines* and *rituals* that reinforce open learning behaviour
- *symbols* that promote open thinking; for instance, key words as humorous reminders on the wall of the effects of closed behaviour and thinking (for instance, Kanter's '10 rules on how to prevent innovation'[3])
- clear *signs* from the leader whether closed thinking is going to be tolerated and *stories* that indicate that strategic learning is feasible.

This can be captured as part of the organization's *learning paradigm* (or 'how we learn (or deny) things around here') as shown in Figure 10.3. The learning paradigm offers the best route to sustaining strategic learning as it enables an organization to become more open and flexible in its learning style. This implies a considerable shift in many reinforcing areas in order for strategic learning to be sustained, rather than isolated attempts to achieve breakthroughs. An example of an intended shift in 'how we learn (or deny) things around here' would be:

	From	*To*
Power relationships	'Strategy is for top management'	'Everyone can contribute to strategic thinking'
Structure (of learning flows)	'Keep new innovation top secret'	'Freely communicate new ideas'
Rewards and recognition	'Punish people for errors'	'Minimize but invest in unavoidable error'

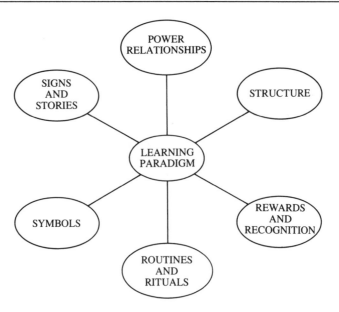

Figure 10.3 How we learn (or deny) things around here: the learning paradigm (Adapted from Johnson, G., 'Strategy, culture and action', in *The Challenge of Strategic Management* (ed. D.F. Faulkner and G. Johnson), Kogan Page, 1992.)

	From	*To*
Routines and rituals	'We never learn much at meetings'	'Our away-days drive change and improvement'
Symbols	'The MD wines and dines on training courses'	'The MD admitted he didn't know and asked if we could help'
Signs and stories	'That was a disaster – he or she is now in Iceland'	'We learned from that success/failure that ...'

One of the key implications of the learning paradigm is that learning (and for that matter other kinds of) intervention may be partially effective. These interventions may rebound off the existing ways in which 'we learn (or deny) things around here'. This suggests that 'outerventions' may often be more effective: here the leader or facilitator tries to draw out of the existing organisational system new patterns of thinking and behaviour, rather than adding new elements.

Interventions and outerventions need not, of course, be mutually exclusive: the key thing is to find an appropriate mix of both.

10.4 The value of strategic learning

Figure 10.4 highlights the value of strategic learning in five key areas:

1. *Time:* being able to move along the time dimension forwards and backwards from past, present to future.
2. *Experience:* distilling and sharing perspectives on organizational experience without barriers or blockages.
3. *Intuitive judgement:* sensing patterns in what is going on and what isn't going on, and why, and what is important versus less important.
4. *Complexity:* understanding the key variables in the business context and in management processes.
5. *Systems behaviour:* discerning patterns in how these variables interact with one another and over time.

These five dimensions of strategic learning help capture some key ways in which value is created or destroyed[4] in organizations, especially:

- in responding to external and internal *change* and in continual *experimentation*
- in coping with *uncertainty* which is driven by systems behaviour (internally and externally), which is both complex and often unpredictable (certainly in terms of linear behaviour patterns)

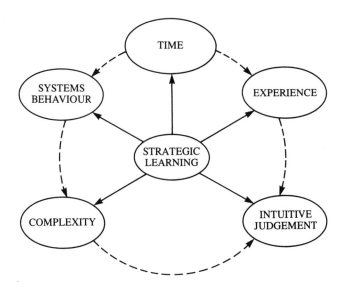

Figure 10.4 Five dimensions of strategic learning

- sensing those variables that have greatest *interdependency* using intuitive judgement and assessing what the impact of that interdependence is likely to be
- helping resolve *ambiguity* through intuitive (but shared) judgement, and testing and refining this judgement.

10.5 Summary

We have explored a large number of issues in this book, beginning with learning and how it can support strategy, and also dealing with implementation, capability and performance. Strategic learning is a process that many leading organizations are seeking to follow implicitly or subconsciously. What this book aims to have achieved is to make this process explicit and deliberate. This should accelerate progress where organizations have begun the journey and may perhaps encourage others to step out.

It also hopes to have distilled and disseminated key lessons through the practice of strategic learning in the cases, through a variety of useful checklists and through the exercises. I hope that you have found the personally based exercises most useful of all.

The still hungry reader may wish to refer to a more comprehensive set of checklists contained in Appendix II. These cover:

- strategic business analysis
- business process analysis
- individual analysis.

To sum up, learning is all about:

L – Leading
E – Exploring
A – Analysing
R – Reflecting
N – Novel ideas
I – Implementing
N – Nurturing (capability)
G – Growth.

It is all of these things, and what strategic learning does is to integrate these within a single unit – with no holes – which makes management easier, not more difficult.

As a final story, consider this:

Once upon a time an enterprising turkey gathered the flock together and, with demonstrations and instructions, taught them how to fly.

All afternoon they enjoyed soaring, reaching new vistas.

After the training was over, all the turkeys walked home.

(Anon.)

Moral: Don't slip back into turkey management.

References

1. Argyris, C., 1991, 'Teaching smart people how to learn', *Harvard Business Review*, May-June 1991, pp. 99–109.
2. Grundy, A. N., *Implementing Strategic Change*, Kogan Page, 1993.
3. Kanter, R., *The Change Masters*, Unwin Paperbacks, 1983.
4. Grundy, A. N., *Corporate Strategy and Financial Decisions*, Kogan Page, 1992.

Appendix I
Case simulation: AZP Services

AI.1 The AZP case

The objective of this case is to enable you to practise strategic learning in a safe learning environment. In the case you will be a fly on the wall. Names are deliberately and obviously fictional to avoid any resemblance to actual organizations. The case is written in a lighthearted style to make it memorable. Another feature is that in the case the characters are somewhat more open and honest about the issues than might be expected in real life. As you will find, their names are deliberately colourful to bring the case to life.

AZP Services is a major division of a European-wide conglomerate called QLG. It is in a number of differing industrial and commercial services as well as having a retail business. Its range of services include:

- Industrial Cleaning
- Industrial Security
- Catering Services
- Retail Dry Cleaning.

These four strategic business units are coordinated by a small divisional headquarters staff based in London. The combined turnover of these businesses is £210 million and profits are £11 million.

Its wide range of products has made the Divisional Board begin to think of 'AZP' as meaning 'A to Z of industrial, commercial and retail products'. Sceptics within the company have coined the opposite view of 'AZP' as meaning: 'Absolute Zero Performance'.

This view of AZP is shared by stock market analysts who have watched earnings stagnate and net operating cash flows decline while the company has grown (until the last two years).

This malaise was aggravated by recession of the early 1990s. Even though, by 1994, gradual recovery is assisting improvements in performance, these are offset by continuing disappointments in many business areas.

The company is run by a relatively autonomous management team who are now under increasing pressure from Group, QLG, to deal 'once and for all' with drifting performance. The new group CEO, Frank Dazzle – a Harvard MBA – made no bones about it at a recent Divisional Board meeting:

> AZP is the embarrassment of Quantum Leap Group (QLG). All our businesses are expected to ramp up their financial performance. Yeah, I have read the text books and know it won't come from me going around beating you up and you going around beating others up, and so on. But, if you don't do something soon and quickly there won't be anything of you all *to* beat up!

AZP's Board directors look as if the world had finally changed for them. They have been half expecting Frank Dazzle to put the pressure on ever since he arrived five and a half months ago from an aggressive US company. The AZP team was made up of:

Divisional chief executive	Toolong Injob
Business development director	Patrick Flash
Operations director	Ralph Actionman
Financial director	Ivor Deskpen
Personnel director	April Sale

The management team (with the exception of Toolong Injob) are new over the past two years – a factor that greatly contributes towards their openness.

The general managers of each of the business units all report to Ralph Actionman. They are based in Holland, Belgium, France and England.

Frank Dazzle left the AZP team to ponder over his imperatives. The mood of the team was sombre. The first to speak was Toolong Injob (CEO).

Toolong: Well, I have to say that Frank Dazzle might be a blessing in disguise. Things are really going from bad to worse and the performance of many of the business units is atrocious. Ivor, what do you think?

Ivor: Yes, I agree, at the risk of upsetting Ralph, just look at last year's annual results:

- Industrial Cleaning (England): making a profit of £2 million on £70 million turnover (down from £3 million).
- Industrial Security (France): making a profit of £5 million on £65 million turnover (down from £6 million).
- Catering Services (Holland): incurring a loss of £1 million on £30 million turnover (breakeven last year).
- Retail Dry Cleaning (Belgium): making a profit of £3 million on turnover of £45 million (up from £1 million last year).

With the exception of Retail Dry Cleaning our performance across the patch is getting worse – and all this is against an improving economic environment. I appreciate, Ralph, we have had problems with quality, cost control and with management across the patch, but with Frank Dazzle on our backs we have to make things really come together.

Patrick: Yes, I can see what the numbers are saying, but all we seem to do in steering the business is play with the numbers. We don't spend half – no, a fifth – as much time in thinking about the changing competitive environment and the critical success factors that we should be focusing on.

Ralph: I believe half of our problems wouldn't exist if we could regenerate our business – especially in Industrial Security and Catering Services. What we need is simpler and better, at lower cost! As you know I have been hammering away at our general managers since I came here fifteen months ago, and although there are signs of some improvement, it is bitty and I do share your concerns, Ivor.

April: Yes, but how do we make it all happen? You don't do any of these things without people understanding where we are, why we have to change, and giving them the skills to change. I don't think we have done nearly enough to communicate what we as a Divisional Board require. Nor have we given the general managers enough support to achieve these breakthroughs.

Toolong: I think this all needs a lot more time to think through. I suggest we organize an away-day to chew over these issues. What I would like us to get out of it is a clear plan of which avenues for turnaround we should explore, both divisionally and business-by-business.

Question 1 (5 minutes)

From what you have gleaned from being a fly on the wall (and using your best imaginative efforts):

1. What key issues underlie the problem of inadequate divisional performance?
2. Do you think the team should try to look at *all* the four businesses on the same day, or just one?
3. Should they cover them *all* at a high level of analysis, then one in depth?

Just six days later the top team reassemble in a local hotel, hurriedly organized by Toolong Injob's secretary. The agenda for the away-day has been set rather loosely – Toolong suggested that Patrick Flash should draw up a number of key questions. These are as follows:

1. What are the real problems that have caused our disappointing performance over the past couple of years?
2. What objectives should we now set that are (a) realistic and (b) fit with QLG's requirements?

Question 2 (5 minutes)

Do you think these questions are sufficiently clear, crisp and well-structured to form a working agenda? If not, what questions would you want to ask?

The directors nervously chink their coffee cups as they wait for Toolong Injob who has been delayed by a traffic jam on a nearby motorway. When he finally appears, they sit down apprehensively. The CEO begins:

Toolong: Sorry I'm late, anyway the traffic jam bought me some useful thinking time. While we inched forward, the thought occurred to me that there were a number of key problems that we should focus on today.

At this point Toolong gets up and draws a 'problem/business' matrix. An engineer by original training, Toolong is fond of drawing pictures to represent interrelated ideas. His artistry is captured in Figure AI.1. The CEO continues:

	INDUSTRIAL CLEANING	INDUSTRIAL SECURITY	CATERING SERVICES	RETAIL DRY CLEANING
QUALITY	☆ ☆	☆	☆	☆
COSTS	☆ ☆	☆	☆ ☆ ☆	☆
SKILLS	☆	☆		

Figure AI.1 Key problem areas of AZP Services (first view)

Toolong: What I have sketched is interesting because it identifies some patterns. Look at Industrial Cleaning and Catering Services, for instance. Both have at least four stars (and Industrial Cleaning actually has five). Now I know we are looking mainly internally here, but it does highlight weaknesses that match the poor financial performance.

Patrick: I agree, but I think your analysis is incomplete.

Toolong: Yes, but my excuse is – the traffic started moving again. You know, it can be as annoying as stopping in the first place if you are in the middle of something like this.

Patrick: One missing piece is our lack of a really clear strategy that will give each business some concrete, competitive advantage. I must say that I find it virtually impossible evaluating new business opportunities that have 'strategic fit' as the strategy of our four business units is so loose.

Toolong: So let's put our 'strategy' up as another problem area, against each business.

April: You can also add into this the issue of management style, which I believe is a major constraint in the business areas of Industrial Security (which seems to be run more rigidly than any company I have come across before) and, to a lesser degree, Industrial Cleaning. I would also question that skills is not an important issue in Catering Services. If you look at their marketing and sales skills, for instance, it really is abysmal.

Ralph: Before we finish, I would like to introduce a sixth element – process simplification. In our larger business units I believe we have major problems in responding to market demand simply because our business processes are so complicated. And they seem to have got worse and not better over the last fifteen months. These organizational weeds seem to have a life of their own. This is a problem in our larger business units.

Toolong: Yes, I've realized that in my second sketch. Put that up too. [See Figure AI.2.] So what does this all mean; how can we bring them all together?

Ivor: Just to show you all that we accountants can use pictures as well as numbers, let me experiment. [See Figure AI.3.]

Ralph: Ivor, I never thought you had it in you – I know some accountants were creative, but this is positively visionary!

Toolong: Yes, I think this is very helpful. I know that we haven't got all the symptoms across all the businesses but we can use this to flush out hidden problems. Also, in both Industrial Cleaning and Industrial Security we could use the full-blown model. Perhaps in Catering Services, too – only 'style' is left out – but I suspect that this is an issue there as well.

April: But at least we can scope down Retail Dry Cleaning, which has a much narrower set of problems.

	INDUSTRIAL CLEANING	INDUSTRIAL SECURITY	CATERING SERVICES	RETAIL DRY CLEANING
QUALITY	☆ ☆	☆	☆	☆
COSTS	☆ ☆	☆	☆ ☆ ☆	☆
SKILLS	☆	☆	☆	
STRATEGY	☆ ☆	☆	☆ ☆ ☆	☆
STYLE		☆ ☆ ☆		
SIMPLIFI— CATION	☆ ☆	☆ ☆	☆	

Figure AI.2 Key problem areas of AZP Services (second view)

Ralph: Before we get sucked into a more detailed analysis, this quick and dirty view certainly seems to have flagged up that three out of four of our businesses need something approaching 'business strategy redesign'. I am for going ahead with this, but do you all realize how much work this will entail? This initial diagnosis suggests a degree of dry rot in the Division that will need some pretty careful and protracted surgery and after-care.

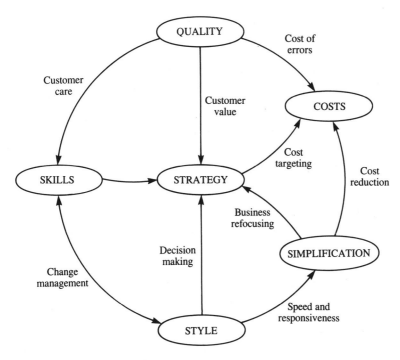

Figure AI.3 Ivor Deskpen's issue map

Question 3 (5 minutes)

At this juncture, what in your opinion did the AZP team do well, and not so well, in establishing a process to embark on strategic learning?

AI.2 Case postscript

The AZP case simulation gives you a preview of some of the issues involved in the use of strategic learning to address organizational capability and performance. It demonstrates again the need to integrate perspectives on strategic issues. This demands a lot of sharing within the management team – and a high degree of openness, which can only occur when people know the true policies of others. Also, individual agendas need to be controlled by the team leader, otherwise they will easily derail any attempts at openness. Strategic learning and strategic leadership are twin elements in creating and sustaining openness.

The problem with maintaining openness is that if it isn't there, you don't necessarily notice its absence. This applies whether you are an insider – where defensiveness is simply taken-for-granted, or an outsider – where you have therefore less intimate knowledge of blocking agendas.

In many ways, the AZP team have sustained an extremely open debate given the apparent severity of the problems and the looming threat of Frank Dazzle, CEO of Group. (Of course, this openness is helped by the absence of the general managers of the four businesses.) Could you be as open in your management team even in facing more minor problems? If you believe that the answer is no, then could you achieve a similar breakthrough, perhaps, by signalling an amnesty on what has gone before?

Also, Toolong Injob, despite the name, seems to have been adept in orchestrating the debate and in facilitating initial thinking. Obviously there are weaker points that need to be listed (to enable you to compare these ideas with your own notes).

AI.3 Suggested answers to questions

Question 1

1. There are a number of possible key issues that might be gleaned from the brief data on the case:

   - competitive positions of one or more of the four businesses might be weakening
   - the businesses may currently be in the process of turnaround by the general managers, and may be able to turn in better results if only sustained effort and patience were applied
   - divisional directors (particularly the operations director Ralph Actionman) may be interfering with operational decision-making by the business's general managers
   - there may be internal, operational or organizational weaknesses undermining profitability.

2. The task of looking at all four businesses in-depth appears to be over-ambitious. Yet management in this case and elsewhere are invariably optimistic about how much they can meaningfully cover in a few days (refer again to the Dowty case in Chapter 5). To some extent, this is probably self-inflicted: deeper down they know that they cannot do justice to the issues in that space of time, but for some reason they feel that strategic learning needs to be rationed. This is often because they don't think through the value that is added if strategic learning is used

effectively, or the value that is destroyed where strategic learning is not done at all.

3. As occurred in the case, it is often more effective to cover a number of businesses first of all at a broad level. This broad view should then be followed by *selective focusing* on 'hot spots' – both business-by-business and on particular issues within such business.

Question 2

The two questions set for the initial agenda were big and rather vague. It is worth while being much more specific (but not over-detailed) in posing key questions to make the learning process effective. A revised list might look like the following:

1. What are the key *external* problems that we have encountered over the past few years?
2. What have we done/not done about them, and with what result?
3. What are the key *internal* problems that we have encountered over the past few years?
4. What have we done/not done about them, and with what result?
5. What overall pattern emerges from the business-specific strengths and weaknesses, and from the strengths and weaknesses of the Division generally?
6. What are the most critical areas for action in which we can achieve a turnaround?
7. How does this match up against expectations of QLG Group?

Question 3

Things that the AZP team did well are:

– take a day out to explore the issues
– have some sort of an agenda
– manage to sustain openness but in parallel with real challenge
– explore the big issues, working top-down without descending into microscopic detail
– try to pick out patterns in the issues
– think about what would be manageable in how turnaround could be tackled.

Things that the AZP team did not do so well are:

– prepare inadequately for the away-day

- not decide formally how, and by whom, the session would be facilitated
- begin with a very broad agenda – in most instances this is a recipe for formless debate and little focused output
- not think about involving the general managers
- not think ahead about whether further sessions would be needed.

Appendix II
Strategic learning checklists

How can strategic learning actually add value in your business, department, role or career? This invites a concluding checklist, which now follows. Can you make a difference through implementing strategic learning in your future? Don't succumb to either mere management fashions or their opposite, cynicism. See if these checklists work for you.

You can now choose from the following checklists and sub-checklists:

- strategic business analysis
- business process analysis
- individual analysis.

AII.1   Strategic business analysis

Strategic business analysis deals with six key areas:

- scenario planning
- competitive position
- strategic choice
- strategic change
- culture change
- business planning.

Scenario planning

1. What key discontinuities does your organization face externally and internally?
2. What different pictures of the future ('scenarios') can you draw up?
3. In what key assumptions (external and internal) are each of these scenarios founded?
4. How important and uncertain are these assumptions?

5. What are the driving forces that underlie the most important/most uncertain assumptions?
6. What is the likely impact on any existing or new strategy, and where?

Competitive position

1. For a particular strategic business unit, how does it add (real and perceived) value to its target customers?
2. How does this compare relative to key competitors within the same, or different, strategic groupings?
3. At what cost is this value achieved relative to competitors?
4. What mutually reinforcing areas of distinctive competitive advantage exist?
5. What makes you think these are sustainable, and at what cost and effort is this achievable?
6. What key sources of competitive disadvantage exist?
7. How important are these, for instance, in terms of losing market share, customer turnover versus retention rates, or unduly high costs?
8. How quick and responsive is the organization in meeting external and internal customer needs?

Strategic choice

1. What is the scope and nature of the businesses in which you operate?
2. What is their competitive position?
3. How (inherently) attractive are their markets and how is this likely to change?
4. What is their desired position?
5. How can this desired position be achieved in terms of choosing to compete in new or more focused ways, or through exploiting emerging market opportunity or niches where others are weak?
6. How likely is it that this strategic choice will be well implemented, given the timing, capability, resources and commitment?

Strategic change

1. Has your company pursued a deliberate versus semi-emergent strategy (building on incremental decision making) in the past?
2. What does an analysis of past and current strategy reveal about the company's *strategic recipes*, i.e. recipes for responding to external change?

3. How is this shaped by the *culture* of the organization and how strong a force is culture in shaping or inhibiting future development?
4. How consistently do current strategy, structure and culture fit together?
5. Is the current direction (in the strategy) well synthesized and communicated consistently either formally or informally by the leader and top management team?
6. Is the organization sufficiently adaptable to meet the challenges of forthcoming change?

Culture change

1. What unique pattern of behaviours, attitudes, beliefs and values forms the hallmark of your organization?
2. Is this culture extremely strong or is there ample scope for individualistic style?
3. How diverse is the culture?
4. How has the culture changed (if at all) over the past five years?
5. What changes are required in the culture over the next five years?
6. What interventions are likely to be needed to shift the culture, or will the desired change happen through natural development and adaptability?

Business planning

1. Is business planning regarded as an essential, living tool used to drive business developments, performance improvement and change in your organization?
2. To what extent is it an open, learning process versus a bureaucratic routine often hijacked for securing political advantage?
3. Do business plans reflect external and competitive needs sufficiently besides internal, operational and financial needs?
4. Are the time-scales, core assumptions and outputs of different plans consistent?
5. Are business plans actually used to prioritize, allocate and reallocate resources in order to secure competitive and financial advantage?
6. Are control, performance review and reward systems all aligned with the business plans?

AII.2 Business process analysis

Business process analysis deals with six key areas:

– critical success factors

- bench-marking
- performance improvement
- quality management
- business process redesign
- operational change.

Critical success factors

1. What does your competitive strategy suggest are the critical success factors (for example, time-to-market of new product launch, achieving a particular market share, achieving the lowest costs in the industry, etc.)?
2. Are these translated into key business, team and personal objectives?
3. Is performance evaluated on the basis of critical success factors and supporting objectives?
4. Are critical success factors well communicated and explained in the organization?
5. Are staff involved in thinking about how these can be most easily met?

Bench-marking

1. Does bench-marking focus on the most critical organizational issues (for instance, as suggested by the critical success factors)?
2. Is it targeted at those companies from which we have most to learn, rather than at those we are merely seeking to beat?
3. Are there clear, targeted and tangible outputs from the process?
4. Will bench-marking try to uncover and compare *processes* rather than merely look at a comparison of output measures (e.g. productivity)?
5. Are bench-marking projects closely and explicitly linked to strategic or more tactical decision-making and change?

Performance improvement

1. What are the key areas of performance groups between actual and desired performance in the organization?
2. Why do these exist (what are the root internal and external causes)?
3. What key options exist for bridging these gaps?
4. What resources and skills are required and will these be made available, and from where?
5. Do processes for monitoring performance against target encourage or suppress learning in the organization?

Quality management

1. Is quality seen as being a strategic issue or purely as an operational or regulatory issue in the organization?
2. Does quality management explicitly link into the competitive strategy and also attempt to create or sustain an open, learning culture?
3. Is a quality management approach applied to a management process, including the making of organic or acquisitive investment decisions, and to business planning and controls and reward systems generally?
4. Is quality management explicitly targeted on measurable goals that will add either direct or indirect business and financial value?

Business process redesign

1. Is business process redesign (BPR) linked directly to the competitive strategy – especially in terms of customer responsiveness and cost reduction?
2. Is it seen as a one-off clear-out of unnecessary clutter and complexity, or is it a continuous process of ensuring that development and change are screened to check that genuine value is being added?
3. Has it become a new ritual or merely an internal product in the organization where it seems to have become an end in itself?
4. What value is unwittingly destroyed by ill-considered pruning?
5. Is management prepared to take its central tenets to the ultimate and consider 'strategy redesign'?

Operational change

1. Are operational changes related to one another as part of a coherent strategy for change?
2. Do they have clear, explicit and well-communicated objectives?
3. To what extent are changes explicitly *project managed*?
4. Are managers prepared to *learn* from the change process or are they unable to do this because of prevailing management style and organizational culture?
5. Are all operational changes cost/benefit analysed and are these assumed cost/benefits revisited as part of the learning process?

AII.3   Individual analysis

Finally, six key applications of individual analysis include:

- Individual competences
- Role analysis
- Personal competitive advantage
- Issue analysis
- Strategic career development
- Managing career transitions.

Individual competences

1. What are your core competences and are there any major gaps relative to current or probable role requirements?
2. What competences should you seek to develop?
3. What development routes might be available both on and off your current job, new job, role enlargement, etc.?
4. What competences are now less relevant to your job and can afford to be harvested (for instance, technical skills)?

Role analysis

1. Why does your current role exist and what value does it add generally?
2. What are the key *processes* through which you add (or possibly destroy) value in your role (for instance, decision-making, people development, idea generation, etc.)?
3. How effective are you personally in each of these processes?
4. Is your role too broad and unfocused to be executed effectively? If so, how could it be suitably refocused?

Personal competitive advantage

1. How much value do you add compared with other managers in your sphere and possibly in other organizations?
2. At what relative cost is this value added, taking into account the resources that you consume either directly or indirectly?
3. How might you sustain your personal competitive advantage through continuous learning and development?
4. Where there are key areas of personal competitive *disadvantage* in your role; does this suggest a major turnaround in areas of greatest disadvantage or even (possibly) a job move?

Issue analysis

1. What key issues do you face in your job over the next 12–18 months?
2. How are these interconnected?
3. Which of these issues is more important/difficult to resolve?
4. Which of these issues is most urgent?
5. Where do the greatest uncertainties lie?
6. Do you need additional resource or support to resolve these issues or can you resolve them by simplifying elements of the problem?
7. Do some of these issues necessitate your managing upwards in order to resolve them as part of wider organizational issues? If so, how will you influence key stakeholders to see it that way?

Strategic career development

1. Given your personal values, aspirations and longer-term ambitions, where do you see your career being in three to five years' time?
2. Where are you now, and what is the gap between where you are now and where you want to be?
3. Are there other options that are both feasible and (possibly) more attractive?
4. How can you achieve career options that more exactly fit your values and needs?

Managing career transitions

1. To what extent is a forthcoming career transition a minor or major discontinuity?
2. What steps can you take to ensure that you don't simply relapse into the routines that have worked in previous roles, but are unlikely to work here?
3. What support can you gain from your boss, subordinates, peers and others to guide you through this transition without your being seen as 'weak'?
4. How long (realistically) will it take to work through?
5. How will you know when you have reached that point?
6. Although you might now see the forthcoming (or current) transitions as a learning process, how can you realistically sustain this?

Index